The Ozarks Spook Light:
History, Legend, and Speculation

Larry Wood

Hickory Press
Joplin, Missouri

ISBN: 9780970282934

Library of Congress Control Number: 2022919421

Published by
    Hickory Press
    Joplin, Missouri

Table of Contents

Preface

In August of 2022, I was visiting with Bob Wolfe at his Always Buying Books store in Joplin (MO) when, knowing that I was a writer with an interest in local history, he suggested that I write a pamphlet or booklet about the famous, nearby Spook Light. I mulled the idea over for a day or two before deciding to give it a go, and the next thing I knew I'd written 30,000 words about the darned thing. Not quite a full-length book but more than a pamphlet, the following pages represent the seed that Bob planted brought to rapid maturity, or at least to adolescence.

The mysterious nighttime light that has appeared on a lonely road near the Oklahoma-Missouri line about five miles south of the Kansas border for many decades has been variously called the Ozarks Spook Light, the Tri-State Spook Light, the Hornet Spook Light, the Joplin Spook Light, and the Quapaw Spook Light. Neosho and Seneca have also claimed the light as their own. In its early days, it was usually known as the Hornet Spook Light, and that is probably still the most accurate designation, since Hornet is the nearest community to the area where the light appears. For the purposes of titling this work, though, I've gone with a broader label to appeal to a wider audience, because the Spook Light's fame is not limited to the Tri-State area. It is known throughout the region and, indeed, throughout the whole country.

Chapter 1
History of the Spook Light

The Early Years

As far as I've been able to learn, the earliest mention in print of the mysterious light now commonly known as the Spook Light, which has been appearing sporadically at night for decades on a rural road near the small community of Hornet, Missouri, is a newspaper article titled "Mysterious Light Puzzles Observers" that was published in the *Joplin Globe* on June 10, 1934. The article described the phenomenon merely as a "strange light on a lonely farm-to-market road, some five miles southwest of Hornet, and approximately sixteen miles southwest of Joplin."

A number of people had witnessed the light in recent weeks and months, but no one knew for sure what the source of the light was. The *Globe* article continued,

> The light…makes its appearance nightly between two groves of trees on an east and west dirt road just east of an intersection called Sixteen Miles and Half Corner.
>
> It seemingly arises from the center of the road and at times gains an altitude of twenty-five to forty feet. It resembles a one-eyed motor car with a bright headlight. At times the light appears in a dim red color not lasting long until it disappears. It can be seen only by spectators looking west on the road. It can best be seen in the center of the road on a clear night.

Except for the assertion that the light could best be seen on a clear night and the lack of wild antics that many later observers attributed to the light, this 1934 depiction of the Spook Light was not that much different from the way people often described it forty or fifty years later. The consensus in later years has been that the light is best viewed on an overcast night, as long as it is not actually precipitating at the time, and apparently the 1934 light didn't alight on any car hoods.

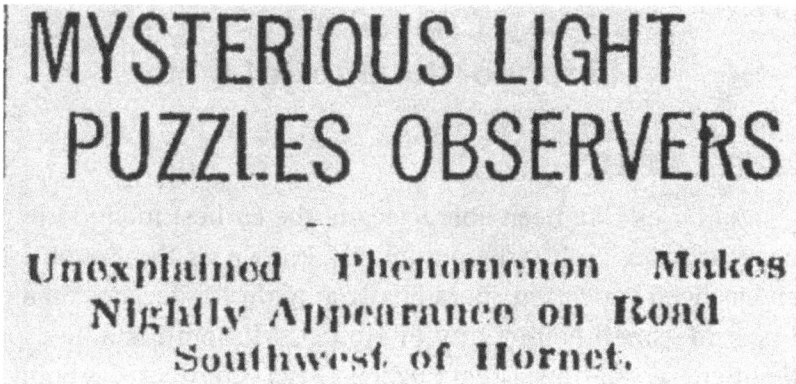

MYSTERIOUS LIGHT PUZZLES OBSERVERS

Unexplained Phenomenon Makes Nightly Appearance on Road Southwest of Hornet.

The mysterious Hornet light was not yet known as the Spook Light when this June 1934 article appeared in the *Joplin Globe*.

The origin of the mysterious light was a subject of debate from the very beginning. The 1934 *Globe* article said some people thought it was caused by the lights of Quapaw, a few miles to the west. Others speculated that it came from lights on a mill or a tailing pile in the Quapaw vicinity, while still others suggested it might be headlights from automobiles as they rounded an S curve just south of Quapaw.

Most residents in the area said they had seen the light for "several years," but one old-timer claimed he'd seen the same apparition appear in the same place for more than half a century.

As news of the mysterious Hornet light spread in the Four-State area, some people took more than a passing interest in the phenomenon. Less than two months after the June 1934 *Globe* article, an Oronogo man, Jim Mase, and a Webb City man, W. Cushman, set out to determine the source of the light. After following the trail of the light from Sixteen and Half Mile Corner to a point about twenty miles east of Coffeyville, Kansas, they stopped at a station, and the station operator convinced them that the mysterious phenomenon emanated from the Coffeyville airport. The strange light near Quapaw, the man told them, was likely a signet light used to direct airplane traffic at the airport south of Coffeyville, over fifty miles away from the Missouri state line.

Y, SEPTEMBER 6, 1934.

ORIGIN OF MYSTERIOUS LIGHT BELIEVED TRACED

A theory of the origin of a strange light, which can be seen on a farm-to-market road some five miles southwest of Hornet, has been advanced by Jim Mase of Oronogo and W. Cushman of Webb City.

Joplin Globe article describes Mase and Cushman's effort to find the source of the Spook Light.

On September 27, 1935, a little more than a year after the *Globe* article appeared, the *Neosho Daily News* likewise took note of the strange Hornet light. "Neosho people are nightly driving up to see the light near Hornet," said the editor. "None have failed to see it so far, and in fact, we have heard it rumored that one girl fainted, swearing afterwards that the light perched on the radiator of her car."

Just a few days later, the rival *Neosho Times* also chimed in on the Hornet phenomenon. In an article that appeared in the October 3 edition of the newspaper, the editor noted that "quite a lot of interest has been aroused in a 'mysterious light' that is said to appear any night on a road that runs west from Hornet into Oklahoma." Many people from Neosho had driven up to the Hornet area at night in recent weeks to see the strange light, but no one had been able to determine its origin or makeup. Several people had driven down the road several miles in the direction of the light but seemingly without coming any closer to it. According to the *Times* article, many people living in the vicinity of the light said it had been appearing for a number of years, while a few elderly residents of the area even said it was there when they were children. The editor had yet to see the light himself, but others had told him it often appeared at first as "a mere speck" that grew brighter before disappearing and then often reappearing a few moments later. "It is said to be so mysterious that it causes a sort of 'spooky' feeling in one who looks at it for some time." This was evidently the first time the word "spooky" was used to describe the mysterious Hornet light, but it would be years later before it became commonly known as the Spook Light.

Advancing a theory that others would later adopt, the *Times* editor said the only logical explanation he had heard for the strange light was that perhaps observers were merely seeing the headlights of distant cars, since the road where the light was viewed was a long, straight stretch and it was known that automobile lights could be seen for several miles in darkness, with the two headlights appearing as one if the distance was even a mile. The varying intensity of the light could be accounted for by how far away the car was, and the disappearing and reappearing of the light could be accounted for by intervening hills or depressions in the road that would obstruct the headlights.

By the end of October 1935, news of the baffling Hornet light had spread beyond the immediate Joplin and Neosho area. For instance, the *Chillicothe Constitution Tribune* told its northern Missouri readers on October 30 that a "weird light" appearing nightly on a country road near Hornet had aroused the curiosity of many observers. Then in late December, *Kansas City Star* feature writer A. B. McDonald trekked to southwest Missouri to observe the light for himself and to talk to people in Hornet, Neosho, and Joplin who'd seen it already.

Perhaps not wanting to be scooped by a big city newspaper, *Neosho Daily Democrat* co-publisher James G. Anderson wrote an extensive article of his own on the mysterious Hornet light about the time of McDonald's visit. Calling the light an "elusive will-o'-the-wisp," Anderson said the crisp winter nights were causing it to appear in its "full brilliance," and several carloads of people had driven out from Neosho to the lonely road near Hornet during the past week to investigate the phenomenon. Without exception, the spectators were able to see the light "dance along the ground" and "lift itself into the trees" while always keeping out of reach.

Anderson said he himself was one of the doubters at first. He thought the whole ado about the mysterious light was silly until he made three separate trips to the site and was able to see the light each time. Although the widespread excitement about the light was recent, Anderson said, the phenomenon had existed for many years. According to legend, Anderson said, the light was the spirit of an Indian chief who had been killed in the area of the light many years earlier. This may have been the first written mention of any legends connected to the Spook Light. We will detail the various legends about the Spook Light collectively in a later chapter.

According to Anderson, a Joplin firm had sent some geological engineers out to the Hornet area several years earlier to investigate the possibility that the light was caused my mineral deposits. The engineers, however, were "at as much of a loss to explain the light as any of us."

All one had to do to see the light, Anderson explained, was to drive slowly down the designated road or park along the road, and within ten or fifteen minutes a light similar to automobile headlights would appear in the distance ahead. Sometimes it could be viewed from one direction and sometimes from the opposite direction, but not from both directions at the same time.

Anderson continued,

> At times the light appears to stand still at a distance of about a quarter of a mile. Then it will creep slowly toward the onlookers until it gets up as close as what appears to be 100 yards. Occasionally it appears up in the trees, then hops down in the road and swings back and forth like a pendulum.
>
> Alternately, it turns three or four different shades of red, yellow, green and white. At one moment it appears as small as an egg.

In an instant it bursts forth in a blinding light almost as large as a football. After shining in this manner for a while it will go out suddenly as if someone had snuffed it out by hand. In a few minutes it reappears as suddenly as it left, often in the opposite direction.

The other night I watched it with a party of five. In order to test the distance, some…watched from the automobile. Others walked toward it. After approaching for a distance of about half a mile, the light still seemed to be about 200 yards distant. No matter how far one walked toward it, it was still just that far away without any appearance of having moved. To the persons sitting in the car it apparently was at the same location as were the ones walking toward it.

Figure out any explanation you wish, but don't scoff. Too many sober persons have viewed it without any appreciable difference in account. One old man in the district says his grandfather told of its appearance there for at least two generations, indicating human agencies were not to blame. Nor could it be the reflection of automobile lights because there were no automobiles back in those days.

Anderson sent his account of the Spook Light out over United Press wires, and it was printed in newspapers throughout the Midwest in late December 1935 and early January 1936. The widespread publicity caused people to travel to the Hornet vicinity from far distances to see the marvelous light. Not everyone who made the trip, however, came away impressed. After Anderson's story about the light appeared in Ralph Cranke's hometown newspaper in Cushing, Oklahoma, Cranke made the 160-mile trip to Hornet to see what all the fuss was about, but he decided right away that the mysterious light was nothing more than the headlights of a car coming over a distant hill and then disappearing as the car got farther down the hill. "They tell you up there in Missouri that the light is a spook that has existed for many years," Cranke told a reporter when he got back home, "but after I first got a glimpse of the light, that was no larger than a baseball, I knew what it was."

When the Spook Light first became well known in 1934, the road running due west from Hornet (now Gum Road), as it approached State Line Road, was the usual viewing area. In other words, the light was seen from the Missouri side of the border. During the thirties and for many years afterwards, the general store at Hornet often served as a jumping-off point for Spook Light seekers. Store owners O. W. "Bud" and Olivia Buzzard directed people to the light and sold booklets about it.

Seen here today, the west end of Gum Road, or a road approximating it, was the primary area for viewing the Spook Light when its existence first became widely known in the early to mid-1930s. *Photo by the author.*

By the time McDonald, the *Kansas City Star* writer, made his trip from Kansas City during the holiday season of 1935, however some folks had already discovered that present-day E 40 Road on the Oklahoma side of the line, about a quarter mile north of Gum Road, was a better viewing spot than the Hornet road. McDonald's feature article, entitled "The Mystery Light of the Ozarks on 'The Devil's Promenade,'" appeared in the *Star* on Sunday, January 5, 1936," and one can discern from the context of the article and other evidence that McDonald and his party viewed the light from E 40 Road.

While researching the article, McDonald was told that the best spot for viewing the light was a rise in the road west of the state line in front of a house owned by a man named Tracey, and he made a trip out to Tracey's place to visit with him one afternoon in early January, preparatory to returning that same night to view the light. Tracey told McDonald he'd bought his home from an Indian couple four years earlier. The couple's two little girls had died not long after the Spook Light made its appearance, and the couple supposedly blamed the tragedy on the light. Tracey said sometimes as many as 100 cars a night lined the road in front of his house trying to get a glimpse of the Spook Light, and there would be 15 to 20 on almost any night.

McDonald left but came back later that night with two carloads of people from Neosho. As the group neared the Tracey place, one young woman in McDonald's vehicle who had "never been out that way before but had been hearing about the light for years" became "too agitated to sit still." She exclaimed, "Oh, I do hope the light will come tonight. I have heard so much about it."

The group parked on the road in front of Tracey's place and waited in a hushed, tense silence for about ten minutes. Then, said McDonald,

> Suddenly in the dark ahead a light bursts into view where all has been darkness. Seemingly, it is detached from any earthly thing and as it hangs in the air it is plainly seen to move toward us, swaying a little this way and that, up and down and sidewise, but always directly above the road and always coming slowly toward us. Then, as suddenly as it had appeared, so it disappears, winks out, and where it had been is only the dark again.

Some in McDonald's group thought the light looked to be only a couple of hundred yards away, while others speculated that it was a mile away. After they waited about five minutes, the light reappeared as a glow right where the previous light had been. McDonald continued,

> This glow always precedes the coming of the light and sometimes the glow appears and no light follows. Looking ahead, along the road, is like looking down a long canyon, the trees on each side giving it this appearance. The glow fills all that gap between the trees and is exactly like the glow I had often seen when driving along a road at night where there was a hill and a car behind the hill was approaching toward its summit, the glow from its headlights illuminating the air above the summit several moments before they came into full view. So this appeared, first a faint luminosity that grew stronger and then the mysterious light sprang into view again, seeming to come toward us

bobbing around as it came, hanging in plain sight for perhaps a minute and then disappeared.

His observations made McDonald think the Spook Light might be car headlights, but one of his companions protested that headlights were two lights and this was only one. So, the group decided to try to get a closer look. Traveling the hilly road slowly west, McDonald and his group never saw the light when they were in the hollows but it always appeared if they waited for ten minutes or so at the crests of the hills. Also, they never saw the light when they looked back to the east, only while looking west.

One person who took note of the excitement over the Spook Light in the mid-1930s was May Kennedy McCord, Springfield journalist known as the Queen of the Hillbillies, whose newspaper column "Hillbilly Heartbeats" was widely read throughout the Ozarks. After briefly recounting the various theories about what the Hornet light was in a May 1936 column, McCord remarked, "I'm sure I don't know, but I'd like to see the critter."

Five years later, Mrs. McCord had still not seen the Spook Light, but she still wanted to. In a July 1941 column, she said she'd recently entertained some guests who "got awfully worked up" about the strange light, and she'd also talked to a young man who'd visited the site just the previous week and watched the light for half an hour. "Believe me," the young man told her, "it's the spookiest, craziest thing I ever saw, and if I had been alone, I believe I would have taken out down the road afoot."

The young man gave his own opinion of the light. He thought it was caused by some sort of bituminous gas that had formed from the deserted mines and chat piles in the area or maybe some sort of phosphorescent mineral. He also told Mrs. McCord there were a lot of other people at the light on the night he and his friends visited it.

"I am simply dying to go," Mrs. McCord concluded, "and always have been. But can never seem to get anyone who wants to go. We may have to make up a party this summer."

In 1942, a group of students from the University of Michigan trekked to southwest Missouri to try to determine the source of the

Hornet Spook Light through scientific tests. Although details about this student expedition are so lacking as to make one question the validity of the story, the group reportedly camped out near the site for about two weeks and even fired high-powered rifles at the light but came away with no definite conclusions.

The University of Michigan group presumably conducted their experiments on present-day E 40 Road, and it was also on this road that later investigations during the 1940s were carried out, including a 1945 inquiry by geologist and mineralogist Dr. George W. Ward and a 1946 study by army personnel from nearby Camp Crowder. All of the scientific and pseudo-scientific investigations of the 1930s and 1940s on present-day E 40, also called Old Spook Light Road, and those of later decades conducted on what is known today as Spook Light Road will be examined collectively in a separate chapter.

E-40 Road is still gaveled today, just as it was in the 1940s when it was the primary spot for viewing the Spook Light. *Photo by the author.*

From the time the Spook Light first became widely known in the mid-1930s, it seemed to hold a special fascination for teenagers and other young people. It was common for hayrides and other youth outings in the Tri-State area to include a stop at the Spook Light. This was still the case when a physics class from Miami High School journeyed twenty miles northeast of town one evening in March 1946 to view the strange phenomenon, not so much to study it but merely out of curiosity. The students came back to Miami and reported there were "too many cars parked around" and they "saw nothing more than a flicker."

In early 1946, C. Paul Spidell of Baxter Springs, Kansas, wrote to the *Kansas City Star* relating an unbelievable experience he'd had with the Spook Light. He described how the light got dimmer and brighter, disappeared and reappeared, "scampered quickly across the field," and then started approaching him in a "wavering dance." It was about ten feet off the ground, and its reflection shone on the hood of Spidell's car. When it was about fifty feet away, it "decided to climb a tree to our right where it perched for a while, losing its brilliance and turning into a sort of "ectoplasmic cloud." Later, the light reappeared and "reproduced itself into three bright little lights with waving arms and leg beams. About six feet apart, the trio scurried through a grove of jackoaks and across a field to our right, then converged into one blazing light" before halting.

There was more to Spidell's story, including a luminous tadpole he'd seen along Spook Light Road, but Charles W. Graham, a member of the *Star* staff, was already hooked, and he was given an assignment to investigate the author's incredible tale. After inquiry revealed that Spidell was a Harvard graduate who seemed to be a practical person not given to fantasy, Graham decided to visit southwest Missouri and northeast Oklahoma to check out the Spook Light for himself. First, though, he wrote to Camp Crowder commander Colonel Dennis E. McCunniff seeking to enlist the US Army in his mission, and McCunniff, intrigued by the apparent mystery of the Spook Light, invited the reporter to come to Crowder and talk it over.

Graham reached the Spook Light area on a Sunday night in early to mid-May of 1946. At first he didn't see the light, but then it appeared, blazing up low in the west at about treetop level. "It turned to red with short flamelike streamers, and winked out." But when he looked over his shoulder, the light "loomed sardonically" over the road to the east. Graham determined the light to his east was just headlights from another car along the road, but his binoculars were not powerful enough to bring the western light into focus. The next day, Graham went to Crowder to seek the army's cooperation in studying the light. The resulting investigation will be detailed in Chapter 3.

Ghost sketch accompanying 1946 Spook Light article in the *St. Louis Star and Times*

By the mid-1940s, the Spook Light was drawing scores of visitors on almost any given night. A St. Louis newspaper described a typical scene at the Spook Light on a summer night in 1946:

> Cars filled with strangers invariably are parked nightly on the backwoods road where "The Light" is a unique attraction. Parties are organized in the spirit of snipe-hunting frolic. But when the jokesters come under its spell, the specter ceases to be sport, and they witness its weird performance with a mixture of amazement and superstition.

Ozarks folklorist Vance Randolph included a section about the Spook Light in his 1947 book *Ozark Superstitions* (later retitled *Ozark Magic and Folklore*). Randolph offered the following description of the light:

> One has only to drive slowly along the road any night after dark to see the "jack-o'lantern" come bobbing along, always traveling in an easterly direction. Sometimes it swings from one side of the road to another, sometimes it seems to roll on the ground, sometimes it rises to the tops of the scrubby oak trees at the roadside, but it never gets more than a few feet from the road on either side.

Saying he'd seen the light three times himself, the author continued,

> It first appeared about the size of an egg but varied until sometimes it looked as big as a washtub. It is hard to judge the distance, but the light seemed about a quarter of a mile off when I first saw it and disappeared when it approached to a distance of perhaps seventy-five yards. I saw only a single glow, but other witnesses have seen it split into two, three, or four smaller lights. The thing looked yellowish to me, but some observers describe it as red, green, blue, or even purplish in color.

Despite the considerable ado about the Spook Light during the 1940s, its heyday, both as a hangout for young people and as a tourist attraction was yet to come.

The Glory Years

Around 1950, what was considered the best area to view the Spook Light switched again, this time to present-day E 50 Road, although the change was gradual rather than sudden. Spook Light viewers continued to use both roads until E 50 finally won out sometime in the mid-fifties as the primary spot from which to see the light. Usually known as Spook Light Road, E 50 is still where most people go today to try to view the light. Around 1949 or 1950, Arthur P. Meadows, who would prove to be the Spook Light's biggest promoter, appeared on the scene. The fact that his appearance roughly coincided with the switch of the viewing area from E 40 to E 50 was probably more than coincidence. He no doubt had much to do with E 50 overtaking E 40 as the most popular viewing spot, because he acquired some land and a small house or shanty on the Missouri side of State Line Road where E 50 comes to a dead end. Meadows set up residency there and began promoting the Spook Light as a tourist attraction. At some point during the fifties, although the exact date seems elusive, "Spooky," as Meadows came to be called, opened a "Spook Light Museum" at the T intersection and put up a sign that read, "Spooksville, U.S.A." A fairly primitive building, the so-called museum sold postcards and other memorabilia about the Spook Light, and it had clippings about the light tacked to the walls. Meadows sold snacks out of the museum, even employing a short-order cook at one point, and most of the "museum" space was devoted to pinball machines, a pool table, and a jukebox. Consequently, the place quickly became a hangout for area youth, and the museum even occasionally hosted dances or other get-togethers for young people, although no drinking was allowed on the premises. Outside on the museum grounds, Spooky set up a telescope looking west along Spook Light Road. He charged visitors a quarter to view the light through the scope.

Although this postcard was still for sale at the Spook Light Museum in the 1970s, the photo may have been taken years earlier by Arthur "Spooky" Meadows, who was once a photographer. *Author's collection.*

The Spook Light itself remained the main draw, of course, and the light continued to be a prime destination for hayrides and other youth activities, whether the outing included a stop at the museum or not. Area churches often sponsored these youth activities. For example, the *Neosho News* reported in late September 1956 that a Seneca Methodist Church Sunday School teacher had taken her class on a hayride to the Spook Light on the previous Friday night.

Even chambers of commerce and other civic organizations got into the act of promoting the Spook Light as a tourist destination, hoping to draw visitors to their respective cities. Both the Joplin Chamber of Commerce and the Neosho Chamber of Commerce published pamphlets or flyers touting the Spook Light as a tourist site. The publication of the Joplin Chamber was a joint effort with the Missouri Division of Resources and Development, and the Spook Light became known by many people as the Joplin Spook Light.

Attendees at conferences or conventions held in the Tri-State area were sometimes treated to tours of the Spook Light. For instance, the program of an Outdoor Writers of Missouri conference held in Neosho in 1956 included an outing to the Spook Light.

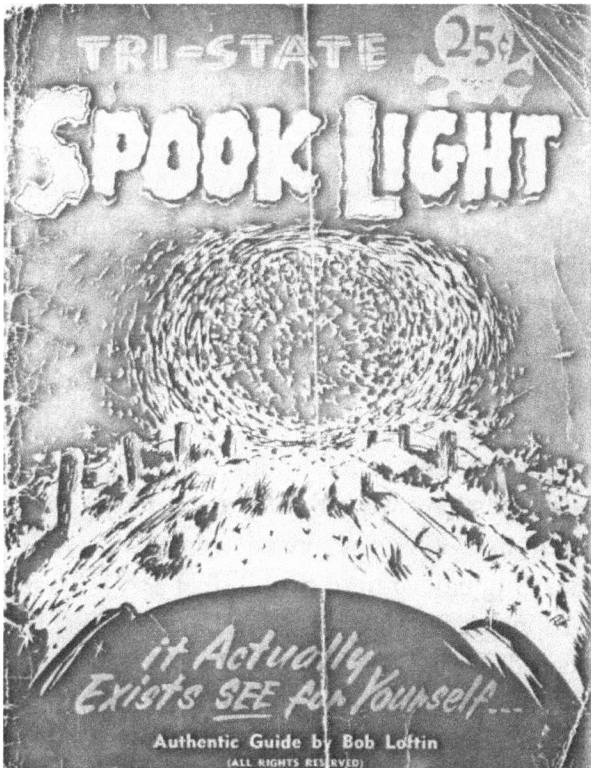

Cover of second edition of Bob Loftin's booklet about the Spook Light. *Author's collection.*

Civic organizations weren't the only ones promoting the Spook Light during the mid-1950s. Joplin resident Robert E. "Bob"

Loftin, a retired military officer who had been interested in the light for several years, also published a pamphlet or "guide" to the Spook Light, and demand for the booklet was such that he later came out with a second edition.

The *Kansas City Star*, which seemed to take a keen interest in the Tri-State Spook Light almost from the very beginning, did an extensive feature story on the phenomenon in October 1955. The reporter, Howard Turtle, interviewed a number of local residents and also offered his own observations:

> The Joplin Spook Light now is attracting a growing number of visitors. It is a "lover's lane" setting, where youths bring their girlfriends, and married couples with their children park to watch the phenomenon. Travelers from afar, visiting with friends and relatives in the vicinity of Joplin or Neosho, invariably are taken out to see the mystery. And seldom does the light fail to put on its show.

When the light made its first appearance on the night of Turtle's visit, it looked "round like a croquet ball, yellow in color." But then another light appeared, "white, ghostly, luminescent—the size of a baseball" that glowed faint rather than bright. At one point, the light changed colors from white to red, and its speed increased to what seemed to the reporter to be sixty miles an hour before suddenly disappearing with a "Whoof!"

Among the people Turtle interviewed was 69-year-old F. W. Mizer. A life-long resident of the Spook Light vicinity, Mizer said he and some his friends saw what he believed was the very first ghost light in the area about 1903 when he was seventeen years old. He described it as a "big ball of light twenty feet across" with a luminous, jack-o-lantern appearance that frightened him and his friends when it suddenly appeared. Mizer said he wanted to run but didn't because his friends didn't, and the light disappeared after about a minute. When numerous sightings of the Spook Light started being reported years later, Mizer figured at first that it was the same type of light he had seen in 1903, but recently he'd decided that the light commonly seen nowadays was, in fact, just headlights, as some people claimed. He said the light he and his friends had seen 52 years earlier was not located in the spot where the modern light almost always appeared. The original light was in a marshy area with lots of cat-tails and similar plants, and he thought it was caused by gasses rising from the decaying vegetation.

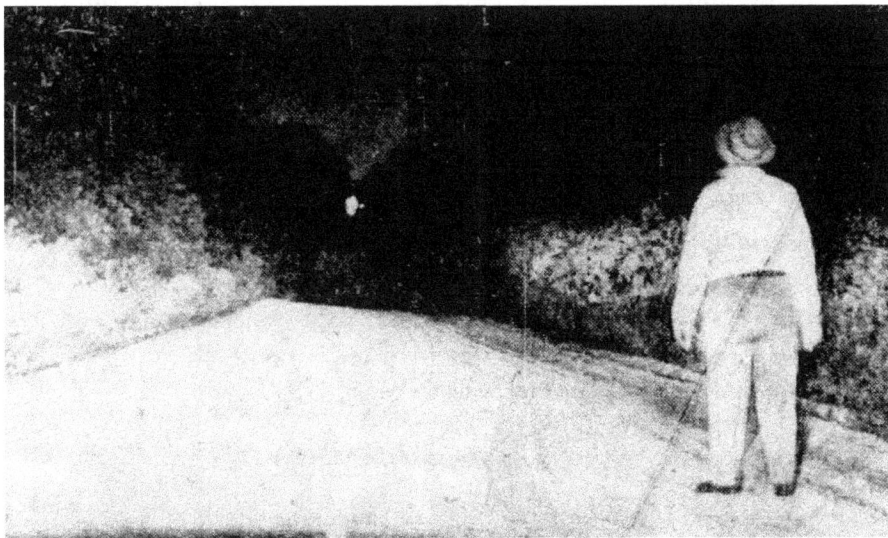

1955 newspaper photo of the Spook Light with Bill Mizer, who said he'd first seen the light in 1903, standing in the foreground. *From the Kansas City Star.*

Turtle found plenty of skeptics of the headlight theory, though, including Lloyd "Dutch" Bilke, who lived a mile east of Spring River and a quarter mile north of Spook Light Road. "I'm 55 years old," Bilke said, "and I grew up in this country, and the engineers can say all they want to about car lights, and I won't argue with 'em, but that light I've seen is no car light." Bilke related an time when he'd seen the light hanging over some oak trees northeast of his place, which put the light in a completely different location from where most people said they saw the Spook Light.

During its heyday, the Spook Light sometimes drew 200 or more visitors a night on weekends. The increased activity and number of people congregating at the Spook Light inevitably led to problems. As early as January 1952, a group of farmers from the Spook Light Road area complained to Ottawa County (OK) authorities about the commotion Spook Light hunters were causing. Disturbances included headlights shining into their homes, the explosion of fireworks, and blaring car horns. The farmers stressed that not all visitors to the area were guilty of such infractions, but they wanted something done about those who were.

One night in September 1954, an 18-year-old Commerce youth suffered a serious knife wound while scuffling with his companions in the Spook Light area. The three young men who were with him rushed him to a doctor in Baxter Springs, from where he was transferred to a Miami (OK) hospital. The injured young man had apparently been wounded accidentally by one of the other boys.

In December 1956, the Ottawa County sheriff announced a crackdown on peace disturbers in the Spook Light area after receiving numerous complaints from area residents of motorists driving at high rates of speed with their headlights off and people shouting in loud voices late at night.

The state of Missouri and other governmental and civic groups promoted the Spook Light as a tourist destination, as this newspaper advertisement from the late 1950s shows. *From the Maryville (MO) Daily Forum.*

The June 1958 issue of *Ford Times*, a travel magazine put out by the Ford Motor Company, carried an article about the Spook Light that only added to its reputation as a tourist destination. The author described the light as "a dull orange glow" appearing in the distance that "floats down the road toward you."

She continued,

It waves from side to side, sometimes large as a bushel basket, sometimes small as an apple. At times there are two or three balls of light, seemingly with wispy fingers extending from them. As the light approaches, you start your motor and put the car in reverse, ready to retreat if it gets much closer. Suddenly the restless light hops to the limb of a small tree, where it burns blue, winking at you like a tiny candle flame.

The article suggested that a visit to the Spook Light could be "a little 'extra' in a tourist's trip to the Shepherd of the Hills country and other parts of the Ozarks. Not every day can a motorist sit in his car and view a living legend. And besides, everyone enjoys a good ghost."

FREE TEENTOWN Ghost Show and Spooklight Museum
SPOOKSVILLE, U.S.A.
10 miles east of Quapaw or 4 miles south of Tollgate on Okla.-Mo. State Line Road.
OPEN 7 A.M. 'TIL 11 P.M.
No Beer or Liquor Allowed

10. HELP WANTED—MALE
FIREWORKS clerks. Spook Light Cafe. 3 miles west of Hornet, then one mile south.

The Spook Light Museum was a hoppin' place for teenagers to hang out in the early 1960s, as these two newspaper clippings from 1961 suggest. *From the Miami (OK) Daily News Record and the Joplin News Herald respectively.*

The halcyon days of the Spook Light continued into and throughout the sixties. In July 1960, Bill Roller, a columnist for the *Tonkawa (OK) News*, recounted a visit he and his family had recently made to the Tri-State Spook Light to the delight of his children. "In years past," Roller said, "I have paid my share of fees to visit some of nature's wonders—balanced rocks, natural bridges, and bottomless springs. Most of them have been worthy of the time, if not the money. But the "Spook Light" belongs to no one. It is visible to any who would take the time to drive to the area—and kids, 6 to 60, will enjoy the experience."

Roller recalled that he'd occasionally visited the Spook Light more than twenty years earlier when he was teenager. He and some of his high school classmates "used to stop in the area to watch the antics of the mystery light. Besides its mystery, your date would invariably sit very close when the eerie light made its appearance."

Roller found it interesting that the location of the Spook Light had changed since he was a teenager. "Whether it is still visible where we used to drive to see it, I don't know. But it is very clearly visible now on Spook Light Road."

Bob Loftin had moved to Tulsa since his booklet about the Spook Light was published in the mid-1950s, but during the early sixties he began work on a revised edition of the pamphlet and made occasional trips back to Joplin to study the light. On one particular night in the summer of 1962, he did more than just study the light. In the wee hours of Saturday morning, July 14, a Newton County deputy got a call that someone was firing a rifle at the Spook Light. Arriving at the scene, the lawman found Loftin in a seemingly intoxicated state, and he had to disarm to the man before bringing him in. Later that day, Loftin was fined $19.00 plus costs and sentenced to five days in jail for disturbing the peace.

While Loftin was working on updating his pamphlet, the Neosho Chamber of Commerce also decided to put out a new brochure about the Spook Light after receiving many calls for information about the oddity. When the new brochure was made available in April 1963 at ten cents a copy, it was in high demand. People came into the office in Neosho seeking the book almost every day, and the Chamber also received several requests a week by mail.

In June 1963, the editors of a new book on Americana announced that they were going to include information about the famous Tri-State Spook Light in the volume.

Later in June, the *Neosho Daily News* reported that there was now a new attraction at Spooksville, in addition to viewing the light.

Spooky Meadows and L. W. Robertson, who had joined Meadows in operation of the Spook Light Museum, were raising a three-legged chicken called Little Angel. Spooky claimed the chicken would sometimes come to him when he called it. "The feed he holds may have something to do with that," the *News* remarked.

In August 1963, Loftin published his revised pamphlet on the Spook Light, and it was well received, at least in Neosho. Both the *Neosho News* and the Neosho Chamber of Commerce touted the new pamphlet, and several businesses in town carried it for sale. The *News* seemed to take issue with the fact that the light was sometimes dubbed the Joplin Spook Light or that Joplin sometimes tried to claim the light as its own. "This is like Oklahoma claiming the Grand Canyon," the newspaper quoted a woman from Tulsa as saying.

During the 1960s, residents of northeast Ottawa County complained of problems caused by sightseers congregating in the Spook Light area, just as they did in the 50s. Among the common complaints lodged by a group of residents in late September 1963 were cars parked in the middle of the road blocking traffic, headlights shining through the windows of residences late at night, people screaming for help when all they needed was help locating the Spook Light, strangers knocking on doors late at night seeking the same information, and beer cans and other trash tossed from cars. Some residents reported mailboxes knocked down or shot full of holes, cattle wounded by gunfire, and petty thievery. A rural school in the area had been broken into twice and property stolen, and in one or two cases private residences had been burglarized while the homeowners were gone. The residents charged that, while some visitors, particularly groups on hayrides, were well chaperoned and caused an inconvenience only by the noise they made, others seemed to come out "clearly bent on mischief." Ellen Clark, the *Joplin Globe* staff writer who interviewed the complaining residents, ended her story on the subject with a list of suggestions for proper etiquette while in the Spook Light area. The list concluded with an admonition to please not shoot at the light, as it might just be a local farmer going about his evening chores and "not a headless squaw out looking for her cow."

An incident that happened less than a year later seemed to bear out the residents' complaints of unruly shenanigans in the Spook Light vicinity. One night in late July 1964, two or three young people on Spook Light Road donned sheets and pretended to be ghosts in an attempt to scare some of their companions. Their disguise, combined with the moans and the other eerie sounds they made, frightened not only their companions but an innocent couple who were parked nearby. The couple retreated to the Spook Light Museum, where they persuaded 32-year-old Albert Shelton to return to the road with them. "When the spine-chilling noises filled the air again," reported the *Kansas City Star*, Shelton started firing birdshot from a .22 caliber revolver in the general direction of the sound. Nineteen-year-old Sam Edwards of Joplin was wounded above the left eye and in the right arm. Edwards, who was treated at a Joplin hospital and released, said he was among those playing the prank and making noise but that he was not wearing a sheet. Meanwhile, the Newton County deputy who investigated the incident turned Shelton over to Oklahoma authorities for legal action, since the shooting occurred on the Oklahoma side of the line.

During the 1960s, the Spook Light attained perhaps even more nationwide notice than it did during the 1950s, because it was written up in a number of big city newspapers across the country. In the spring of 1963, a UPI story about the light appeared in several city newspapers, including the *Oklahoma City Daily Oklahoman* and the *Cincinnati Post*. Bearing a date line of "Spooksville MO," the article said, "This town is marked by a small store, a dead-end intersection, and a 'spook light' across the stateline in Oklahoma." Also in 1963, Los Angeles resident Raymond Bayless, an amateur researcher and investigator of psychic phenomenon, made a trip to Missouri and wrote up an extensive report on his study of the Spook Light. In March 1964, a columnist for the *Los Angeles Times* reviewed Bayless's report and wrote about the mysterious Missouri light.

In 1966, a *Chicago Tribune* columnist, after reading a brochure that claimed the Spook Light had been around since 1886, conducted a telephone interview with Spooky Meadows and Warren Harmon, whom he called co-curators of the Spook Light Museum.

(Actually, Harmon just helped out there for a while during the sixties.) The result was a tongue-in-cheek story about the light that appeared in the June 16 edition of the *Tribune*. According to the columnist, the Spook Light was located about halfway between Joplin and Seneca, Missouri, "which is not an unreasonable place for a spirited ghost to take up residence."

Both Meadows and Harmon thought the light was "pretty mysterious," the columnist added. "O, of course, scientific fellows have come snooping around, and some of them have said it is the reflection of lights from Route 66, 18 miles away. This is not held too likely by Messrs. Meadows and Harmon, as the automobiles traversing 66 in 1886 were fairly meager."

The Chicago scribe said Harmon told him proudly that the museum featured a coin-operated pool table, a shuffleboard, a rifle range, pinball machines, and a jukebox. "Very few spook lights are surrounded by modern conveniences of this kind," the columnist remarked.

A book entitled *Mysterious Fires and Lights*, published in 1967 by the David McKay Company of New York, included a write-up about the Spook Light. The author, Vincent Gaddis, said the light had almost attained "the status now of a tourist attraction."

In early 1968, a reader wrote to the *Joplin News Herald* asking the "Trouble Shooter" columnist whether the Spook Light was "still going." The answer: "Troubleshooter wishes to advise that if the spook light was ever there it still is."

In 1968, Bob Loftin published a book entitled *Identified Flying Saucers*, and one section concerned the Spook Light. I'll discuss Loftin's take on the light, as expressed in this book, in more detail in Chapter Three, but suffice it to say here that his view had evolved, or rather undergone a revolution, since he'd originally published his little pamphlet on the light in the mid-1950s.

As Halloween of 1969 approached, *Joplin Globe* writer Ron Bogue interviewed Arthur Meadows, or "Spookie" as Bogue called him, for his "Around the Globe with Bogue" column, and the resulting story was published on October 30, the day before the ghostly holiday.

"Spook lights appearing, but this old man is disappearing." That's the first thing Meadows said when the interview officially got underway at the Spook Light Museum about eleven miles southwest of Joplin. He was referring to the fact that he was getting old and would soon have to turn over the museum operation to somebody else. Spookie, who was getting ready to turn 75, lived alone at the museum. "I just camped here one day, and I've been here ever since. It's the only home I've got. And besides, someone needs to be here to answer people's questions."

Spookie offered to sing a song he'd written about the Spook Light, but it's not clear whether Bogue took him up on the offer. Reflecting on his many years running the Spook Light Museum, Meadows said, "I haven't done this to make me rich. But there's possibilities here. It's a wonderful attraction. There ain't nothing like it in the world."

Spookie said his property on Spook Light corner consisted of 25 acres, and he daydreamed about selling it to someone who might develop it into a full-fledged tourist attraction called "Spook Lights City." But Spookie said he was getting too old even to run the museum in its current condition, and his friend Garland Middleton, who lived not far away, opened up for him each evening.

"Spook light's here, but this old man is disappearing," Spookie repeated as the interview ended. "It's here and it's gonna stay."

Garland Middleton took over the museum full-time shortly after this, and Arthur Posey "Spooky" Meadows died less than two years later. In addition to taking over operation of the museum, Middleton also inherited his predecessor's nickname, Spooky.

Although interest in the Spook Light as a tourist destination and as a youth hangout may have peaked during the sixties, hundreds of people per week continued finding their way to the isolated spot on the Missouri-Oklahoma border to view the strange phenomenon throughout the seventies, and the Spook Light Museum still thrived, at least as a curiosity, under the management of Spooky Middleton.

In July 1971, Mike Kelley, a staff writer for the *Springfield Leader-Press*, recalled his growing-up days in the Joplin area:

One of the popular pastimes for a Joplin youth about the time I was reaching adolescence was the church—or privately—sponsored hayride, which inevitably toured the Spook Light.

Well, sometimes these groups of youngsters saw the Spook Light, and sometimes they didn't. But there was usually more sparking beneath the blankets, which the girls always brought along on the chilly fall nights, than spooking. Many a young couple got its sex education on a hayride, ironically sponsored by a Baptist Church.

In May 1972, New York City resident Sabra Elmore, who, like Kelley, had grown up in Joplin, wrote a feature article for the *Joplin Globe* recounting the first time she'd seen the Spook Light as a high school student in the early 1950s. "The vogue at that time," she said, "was to get your boyfriend, several other 'going steady' couples and somebody's dad's car and head for Hornet, Mo., to see the 'Ghost Light.'"

Continuing in her lighthearted tone, Ms. Elmore added,

We had everybody picked up by nine o'clock…giggling and talking about how scared we felt and how spooky it was going to be…. We really didn't have to pretend to be spooked because there is something about an isolated gravel road in Missouri that speaks for itself.

When the light first appeared, Sabra and her companions found it hard to breathe and "we couldn't speak…. No more joking about how there isn't any such thing and how it has to be someone walking along with a lantern or maybe it's a ghost looking for its head…. That shimmering blob was about five feet off the ground and just staying in one place.

After staring at the light for a while, Sabra and her friends got out of the car and walked down the road hand-in-hand "protecting each other from God knows what" and teasing each other about how frightened they were. "While we were being cute and daring," Sabra added, "we had forgotten to keep our spying eyes on the object of our witticisms." When the group thought to look up, the Spook Light was gone, and they turned to go back to the car. They stopped short when they saw the light was now about ten feet behind them and they had not seen it pass. "Needless to say, that ended the excursion for the evening because we fled to the car and roared home in a huge cloud of dust that only two car washings would take off."

From an Actual Photograph of the Mysterious Spook Light
seen regularly between Joplin and Seneca, Missouri
Garland Middleton

Postcard photo of the Spook Light from the 1970s, by Garland Middleton. *Author's Collection*

In October 1973, freelance writer Willard Rand trekked to Joplin to do a story on the Spook Light for the *Kansas City Star*. He found a young man at a Joplin motel, Dave Shaw, who agreed to accompany him out to the Spook Light and show him where it was. Shaw's girlfriend declined to make the trip, saying she was too scared. After a stop at the "Free Spooklight Museum" and a brief visit with Spooky Middleton, Rand and his companion parked on Spook Light Road several hundred yards west of the state line. Darkness set in and Rand had just begun to feel a bit foolish when the light "popped on." It was in the center of the road at a distance of what seemed to Rand to be about 100 yards. "It wavered, grew bright as an electric lantern, danced a bit, flicked off."

When the light reappeared, it was "as big as a baseball and ghostly white," according to Rand. "It wavered about and burned for what seemed like a minute, then it shot off the right and disappeared. At times it would look like a lantern carried by someone slowly walking. Then it appeared to be a ball of fire hurtling at us with great speed—only to stop, bounce around near tree top level and zoom back into the distance."

Rand offered no opinion on what he thought the source of the Spook Light might be, but he closed with the following observation:

> There in the scruffy hills of the Ozarks where ghost stories are as thick as ticks in a jimsonweed patch, all it takes to be frightened is imagination and some nervous companions. One can read into the light almost anything he wishes. It is usually more fun for people to assume the light is a specter.... Or it could be an old fashioned flying saucer—or any of the half dozen stories the local Mark Twains dream up.

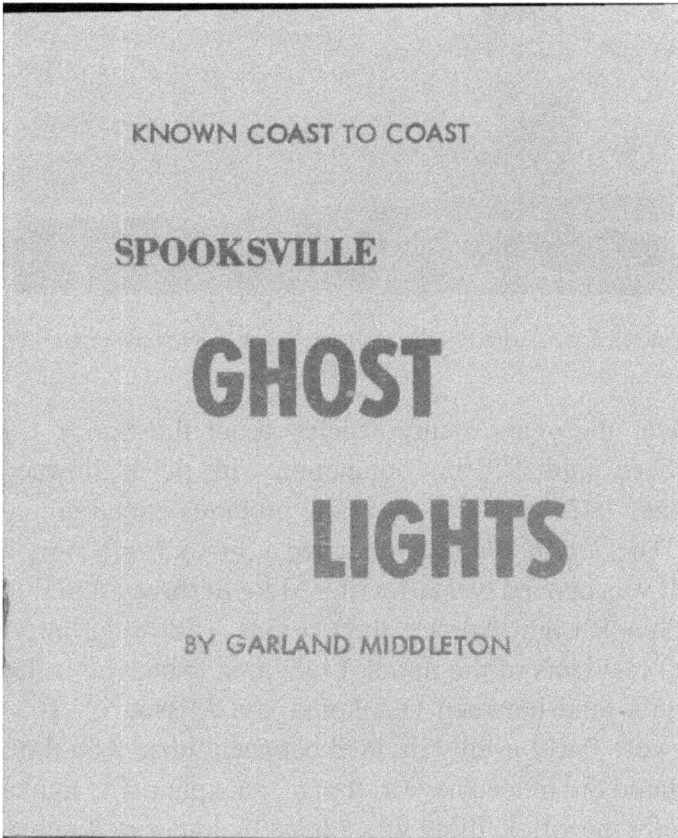

KNOWN COAST TO COAST

SPOOKSVILLE

GHOST

LIGHTS

BY GARLAND MIDDLETON

Cover of a Spook Light booklet compiled by Garland Middleton that was among the memorabilia sold at the museum during the 1970s. *Author's collection.*

The October 1976 edition of *Ozark 71*, a guidebook to what was happening along US Highway 71 (now I-49) between I-44 and I-40, included an article about the Spook Light entitled "Ghost Light of the Ozarks." The article claimed that "only the very bravest have ventured into the area at night and waited for the pixyish light to waver into view," before recounting some of the legends associated with the Spook Light and mentioning a few of the investigations of the light that had been done.

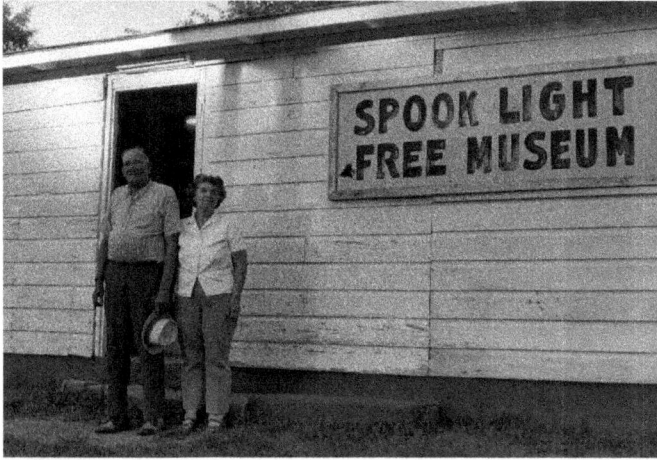

Spooky Middleton and his wife, Hazel, outside the Spook Light Museum, circa 1976. *Photo by the author.*

Over the years, many articles about the Spook Light have fittingly been published in conjunction with the Halloween season. The October 1976 article cited in the previous paragraph is just one example. The *Joplin Globe* also carried a Spook Light story in the fall of 1976. It was penned by staff writer Mike Surbrugg and titled "Hoax or Real, Spook Light Attracts the Curious." Surbrugg interviewed a number of residents of the Spook Light area, which he called "a type of no man's land between Oklahoma and Missouri." The folks he spoke to were fairly evenly divided between those who thought their neighborhood did indeed have a strange, unexplainable light and those who thought the whole thing was a hoax that appealed only to people who wanted to be fooled. Some told tales of eerie encounters with the light, while others said they'd lived in the area their whole lives and never seen the so-called Spook Light. What nearly all the residents agreed on was that curiosity-seekers congregating in the area and behaving sometimes in an unruly manner was a definite nuisance. Speaking of Spook Light Road, one resident said, "Everything imaginable goes on down that road every night of the week. It's unbelievable."

In March 1977, two men from the North American UFO Organization arrived in the Joplin area to study the Spook Light, and *Joplin Globe* staff writer Marta Poynor did a feature article outlining their investigative plan and briefly describing the antics of the light. The *Globe* published, in conjunction with the article, an unusual photograph taken by Ms. Poynor, showing the light as a big glowing ball with a smaller ball shooting off from it.

Spook Light Museum, circa 1977. Author's collection.

The rowdy behavior that frequently plagued the Spook Light area sometimes crossed the line into criminality. On the night of March 27, 1980, a man tried to take some money by force from Garland Middleton at the Spook Light Museum, but the old codger fought off his assailant and the would-be robber retreated. A thirty-year-old Joplin man was arrested a few days later in connection with the incident and charged with attempted second-degree robbery.

The photo on this page and the ones on the previous page were taken minutes apart on an evening in 1977 against a backdrop of progressively darkening skies. *By the Author.*

An article called "A Special Spooky Road" appeared in *The Ozarks Mountaineer* in July-August 1980. Drawn by a legend she had heard about young, Native-American lovers who leaped to their deaths in a suicide pact from a bluff overlooking Spring River, author Evelyn Sanders chronicled her family's frightening first visit to Spook Light Road. She described her emotions when the light first appeared, hovered above a "cow pasture…for what seemed like ages," and then started toward her family:

> I can't express the ineffable presence I felt in that moment. My ears rang with wild vibrations as though someone was desperately crying for help, and I was shackled. My eyes blurred with anxiety. What if the lovers sought revenge? Apprehension sent my heart pounding. My throat drained of saliva. I knew I couldn't run if my life depended on it!

A feature story about the Spook Light also appeared in the *Kansas City Times* in 1980, the day before Halloween. For the article, the writer interviewed a Kansas City outfitter, Robert Hoenike, who for years had led groups on camp-outs to the Spook Light area. Hoenike said he didn't believe the legends behind the light but he did think the supernatural played some part in the light. "I've tried putting people in front of it and behind it," he added, "and put some on both sides of the road, but it just jumps away. It defies explanation."

In the spring of 1981, a crew from NBC's *Real People* television show came to the Neosho-Joplin area in preparation for the airing an episode about the famed Spook Light. The NBC folks interviewed a number of area people who were knowledgeable about the Spook Light, including Crowder College physics instructor Herb Schade, as well as everyday people who had seen the light. As a freelance writer who had published several articles about the Spook Light, I, too, was contacted by an NBC representative to get my perspective on the light for the upcoming episode. My wife still teases me sometimes about the phone call I received from "Miss Monique." The *Real People* episode about the Spook Light was scheduled to air on October 26, 1981, just in time for Halloween, but it was reset for December and didn't finally air until 1982.

UPI writer Paula Maynard also wrote a story about the Spook Light in 1981, and it appeared in various newspapers across the country in late October. In pursuit of the story, Ms. Maynard and a guide had driven three hours south of Kansas City and then "five bone-jarring miles down a gravel road" to reach the Spook Light on a Sunday night. "A dozen vehicles jammed with spook seekers saw fit to join us that very night," she related. "Cars and customized four-wheelers zipped along, tossing beer cans, revving engines, flashing head, tail and running lights. Not my idea of an atmosphere to lure a lonesome spook."

Ms. Maynard said she was starting to realize the silliness of straining to see a tiny twinkle in the distant darkness while ignoring the "glittering canopy of stars overhead" when the Spook Light finally made its appearance. Viewing it through binoculars, she described it as a light that "peeks out of [a] V-shaped notch where the Blackjack Oaks and the road come together against the sky."

The reporter thought the glowing orb could be headlights from a distant road, as some had theorized, but she wasn't sure, especially after the light disappeared and then reappeared, "shrinking smaller as it came nearer until it more resembled a cigarette than a headlight."

As Ms. Maynard and her guide turned around to leave, the light pulled its "peek-a-boo" routine again, but "it bounced on without us."

Still keeping with the Halloween theme, on October 31, 1981, the *Pittsburg Morning Sun* carried a story by staff writer Max McCoy entitled "Elusive Spooklight—the Mystery Lives On." After witnessing the light as a brief flicker at the west end of Spook Light Road and recounting some of the legends and theories behind the light, McCoy concluded that the atmosphere along the dark, tree-lined road was "certainly conducive to seeing *something*."

In late November 1981, *Joplin Globe* staff writer Joannie Kidder did a story about the Spook Light or, more specifically, a profile of Garland "Spooky" Middleton, curator of the Spook Light Free Museum. Dressed in his characteristic bow tie, the 72-year-old Middleton perched atop the pool table in the middle of the museum's main room to speak to the reporter. Thinking perhaps that Ms. Kidder might wonder how a person could make any money running a ramshackle "museum" like his in an out-of-the-way rural setting, Middleton answered the question before she could ask it. "Why, at my age and my wife's age, when we both get Social Security, why would I want to make any money?" Spooky asked rhetorically. "I'd just have to leave it to somebody.... Actually, the way I'm hooked up here, it's a hobby. I can't make any money this way.... It's worth it to me to show these people around and tell them about the spook light."

Middleton said the most visitors he'd ever had in one night was 271, although the average range was 20 to 125 a night. He kept the museum open four or five hours a night, six nights a week, all year long. He said he'd only lost 25 nights to bad weather during the 13 years he'd run the place. Sometimes they came in by the busload. After looking over the fading clippings on the walls and the sparse furnishings of the museum, Ms. Kidder concluded that the people didn't come for the museum artifacts but for "the man who perpetuates the legends."

Spooky said he didn't keep much money on the place for fear of robbers. Relating the encounter he'd had a year and a half earlier with the would-be robber, he said the man hit him twice in the back of the neck as the two were walking toward the door together, and the blows knocked Spooky down. Realizing his assailant did not have a gun, Middleton decided to put up a fight. As he got to his feet, he knocked the intruder "halfway over to the pool table and hit him three or four licks while he was coming up."

The attacker was much quicker than the older man, but Spooky was able to neutralize his foe's advantage by getting him in a clench until he could regain his breath. Finally, the scuffling pair fell through the door and landed outside, and the wanna-be robber took off running when a car happened by about the same time. Spooky lamented the fact that the man later got off with just a parole.

Middleton was starting to think about the time when he would have to quit running the museum, but he wasn't looking forward to it. Spooky said he'd acquired the museum because it "was in the family." He explained that he and Arthur Meadows had married sisters, and he'd traded his "kinda related" predecessor an old Plymouth and some cash for the place. Middleton said he wanted to keep the place open for poor folks who needed a source of cheap entertainment.

Although his interview with Joannie Kidder served more or less as Garland Middleton's farewell to the Tri-State area, he wasn't quite ready, as Spooky Meadows had been at the time of his exit interview in the late sixties, to fade away. Meadows's motto, "Spook lights appearing, but this old man is disappearing," didn't fit Spooky Middleton.

But it wasn't long before he was reconsidering his determination to stay on at the museum. Perhaps an incident that happened six months later hastened his change of heart. In early June 1982, someone broke into the museum, stole a case of beverages and several packs of cigarettes, ransacked the office, and damaged the coin boxes in the pinball machines, the pool table, and the jukebox. Spooky was still running the museum four months after the break-in, when *the*

Kansas City Star ran a brief story about the Spook Light during the 1982 Halloween season that focused mainly on telling readers how to get there, but maybe the 73-year-old man was getting tired of dealing with robbers and burglars. He closed the museum for good on August 31, 1983, and he died in early January 1984.

The Spook Light Loses Its Luster

The Spook Light, at least as a tourist attraction and a hangout for youth, entered a period of slow decline after Spooky Middleton closed the museum and no one stepped forward to take it over. Several factors contributed to the waning interest. The closure of the museum itself was perhaps the main one. Without Spooky there to regale people with stories about the light, a visit to Spook Light Road just wasn't quite the same. The paving of Spook Light Road and State Line Road a few years later also lessened the eerie atmosphere. The whole Spook Light area didn't seem quite as spooky or rustic after the roads were paved as it did when the roads were graveled. Increased law enforcement in the area and too many modern-day activities competing for people's attention also likely had something to do with the decline in interest in the Spook Light as a quaint attraction. Another probable cause, which is hard to ignore, is the simple fact that sightings of the Spook Light became rarer than they used to be.

Evidence of the declining interest in the Spook Light as a source of entertainment is the fact that noticeably fewer articles about the light as a tourist attraction or a destination for a fun-filled adventure have appeared in print during the past forty years than appeared during the previous forty. Only a handful of general, informational articles extolling the simple mystery and charm of the Spook Light, as most of the articles published in the old days did, were published during the first decade and a half after the museum closed. One was an article that came out in *The Chart*, Missouri Southern State University's student newspaper, in September 1983, just a month or so after the museum closed. The article described some of the legends and theories about the Spook Light and concluded that it would probably continue to be a source of amusement and entertainment for generations to come. *In. Joplin!* magazine published two separate articles about the Spook Light in the mid-1980s, and a short article about the phenomenon was included in a book entitled *Haunted Heartland* that was published in 1986. But that was followed by a ten-year dearth of Spook Light articles.

Then, starting in the late 1990s, a few additional articles about the light were published in a rather short span. During the Halloween season of 1997, the *Los Angeles Times* carried a story by AP writer John Rogers describing the antics of the Spook Light and recounting various people's encounters with it. In 1998, Show Me Route 66 printed an article about the Spook Light relating some of its history and legends and recalling the strange encounter Dutch Bilke had with the light as a young man, the same experience Bilke had told the *Kansas City Star* about in 1955. In July 2003, the *Missouri Conservationist*, a publication of the Missouri Department of Conservation, printed an article about the Spook Light by Joplin-area writer Suzanne J. Wilson describing her own experience with the Spook Light and those of several other people she interviewed. Recounting her own group's reaction when they first saw the light, Ms. Wilson said,

> We're bobbing and weaving, seeking vantage points, looking through binoculars and a six-inch reflector telescope. What we watch for the next hour is a conglomeration of light that waxes and wanes, disappears and reappears. Full of surprises, it shimmers, or looks like a necklace of lights or shrinks to mere twinkles…. It's far away, but how far?

On Halloween day of 2004, the *Joplin Globe* published an article about the Spook Light by Kay Kirkman describing the Spook Light and recounting some of the various explanations for it. There may have been a couple of other general articles about the Spook Light printed during the past forty years that I've overlooked, but the half dozen or so mentioned above are the main ones I've come across. I should also stress that I have concentrated my research on print sources and have not attempted a comprehensive review of the plethora of stories about the Spook Light that have popped up online during the Internet age. Many of the online articles are just rehashes of previously printed stories and legends, but a few are serious contributions to the Spook Light literature.

As recently as 2018, Noel native and filmmaker David Glidden showed a documentary about the Spook Light at the Route 66 Theater in Webb City. Around the same time, Joplin resident Josh Shackles led ghost tours that included visits to the Spook Light.

And just last year (2021), Curtis Almeter did a story about the Spook Light for the *Joplin Toad*, but Almeter came away disappointed when he failed to see the light.

So, don't get me wrong when I say there has been a decline in interest in the Spook Light. I'm not suggesting that curiosity about the light has disappeared. Interest in the Spook Light persisted long after Spooky was gone, and it has continued until this very day. It's just not as strong as it once was.

Also, there is one notable exception to my observation about the decrease in interest in the Spook Light and the decline in published articles about it. Scientific and pseudo-scientific investigators seeking to discover the source of the light have been even more prevalent since Spooky Middleton left the scene than they were in the early days of the Spook Light, and many published articles in recent years have focused on these investigations, as opposed to earlier articles, which tended to focus on the light simply as a curious attraction. These recent investigations and those of earlier researchers will be detailed in Chapter 3.

Chapter 2
Legends Behind the Spook Light

According to a story handed down by word of mouth, when the Spook Light was first sighted in the late 1800s, it caused such panic in the small community of Hornet that many residents packed up and moved away. Among those who left were a Native American couple who blamed the "evil light" for the deaths of their two children.

A number of supernatural legends purporting to explain the origin of the Spook Light were also handed down or else developed very soon after the light became widely known.

Likely one of the first was the story of the Devil's Promenade. According to legend, if the old, wooden bridge over Spring River was crossed a certain number of times or was crossed too many times, the Devil would appear. Thus the bridge became known as Devil's Promenade Bridge, and the light was thought to be an evil omen. Although a modern bridge has replaced the old wooden one, the structure still bears the name Devil's Promenade.

Another old and persistent legend, one that involves a young Native American couple of different tribes who fell in love and planned to marry, is also related to the Devil's Promenade, and it is even better known than the basic bridge story. According to this tale, when the young maiden's father, who was chief of the Quapaw tribe, thwarted the marriage by demanding an unusually high payment for his daughter's hand, the ill-fated lovers ran away together, but the old chief sent his warriors after them. Fearing severe punishment if they were caught, the young couple grew despondent and leaped to their deaths together from a large rock or bluff overlooking Spring River near the Devil's Promenade Bridge. Often called Lover's Leap, the bluff itself is sometimes referred to as Devil's Promenade as well. In fact, even though the river and the bluff are located a few miles west of the area where the Spook Light is normally viewed, the Devil's Promenade has lent its name to the entire Spook Light area. Spook

Light Road, in particular, is often called Devil's Promenade, and the light supposedly shines as an eternal symbol of the young couple's love for each other.

L
1955 newspaper photo of Lover's Leap (sometimes called the Devil's Promenade) on Spring River a few miles west of the Spook Light area. *From the Kansas City Star.*

A less well-known Quapaw legend holds that one night in the 1800s or very early 1900s, a woman who had "bewitched" some Indian children was walking by herself in the woods carrying a lantern. An Indian riding horseback lost control of his mount, and the animal ran over and killed the witch as she walked along with lantern in hand. Her ghost continues to haunt the Spook Light area.

Another Native American legend says the Spook Light marks the spot where a band of Cherokee Indians, racked by hunger, disease, and exhaustion, were forced to sell their women and children into slavery near the end of their journey along the infamous Trail of Tears in 1836. The Spook Light glows as an endless reminder of the cruelty of that forced removal of the Cherokees to Oklahoma from their ancestral homelands in the Southeast.

Other Native American lore suggest that the light is the ghost of an Osage chief who was murdered in the Devil's Promenade vicinity or that it is the spirit of a Quapaw maiden who drowned herself in the river after her warrior was killed in battle.

Another interesting legend about the light holds that a Civil War sergeant was leading a squad of soldiers with orders to seize and burn several mills along Shoal Creek in northern Newton County when his detachment was captured by the defending forces. Being well known to his captives for his cruelty to prisoners who'd fallen into his hands, the old sergeant was ordered shot by cannon fire rather than the usual firing squad. He was tied to tree stump, and the cannon fire completely decapitated him. His head, considered a valuable trophy, was hunted for hours but was never found. The legend claims that the sergeant was too tough to kill and that he freed himself from the stump and somehow found a lantern. He went looking for his head and is still searching for it to this very day.

Another folktale says that the children of an early-day miner were kidnapped by Indians while the miner was at work. Upon returning home after dark, the miner found the children gone and set out looking for them with lantern in hand. He is still looking for them to this day. A variation on this tale is that an old miner, carrying a lantern across a field toward his house, disappeared and is still trying to find his way home. Another version of the story is that the small daughter of a miner wandered away from home one night and was never heard from again, and she still walks the countryside every night with lantern in hand looking for food. A ghoulish variation on the miner's story claims he came home drunk one night and threw his baby into the fireplace. His wife waited until he was asleep and then cut off his head with an ax. The miner has been looking for his head ever since, and the Spook Light is the glow of the lantern he carries.

Long ago, a moonshiner used the rugged region of northeast Ottawa County as a hideout for his still, according to another strange tale. He moved the still every so often to avoid revenuers, and when the Spook Light first appeared years later, old-timers said it looked just like the now-dead moonshiner's wagon bouncing down the road.

In addition to the superstition that the light is an evil omen from the Devil, a similar legend holds that it is a benevolent sign from God.

A relatively modern Native American legend that is related to the Spook Light but doesn't purport to explain it holds that an Indian was riding his motorcycle along the road one night when the light appeared and frightened him so much that he fell off his cycle and was killed.

Chapter 3
Scientific and Pseudo-Scientific Investigations of the Spook Light

Just as supernatural legends purporting to explain the Spook Light were put forth from the time the phenomenon first became public knowledge, so, too, did scientific-minded individuals attempt to solve the mystery of what caused the light.

Shortly after the light became known, geologists suggested it might be an electrical emanation from ore buried in the ground. About the same time, a civil engineer from Joplin came out to the light and set up with a surveyor's transit to try to measure the distance to the light, but the trees on both sides of the road were so thick that he couldn't get a good measurement. Two amateur surveyors from Neosho, F. H. Darnell and Joseph Duck, also came out to the site with a transit, but the light was in view for such a short time and bobbed around so much that they couldn't center it in the crosshairs.

When James Nutz and Raleigh Carter, two Joplin men, first heard about the light in the early to mid-1930s, they went out to the site with powerful binoculars and looked at the light through the glasses. They concluded that it was a light on top of a gravel pile at a zinc mine on the west side of Quapaw. When it was pointed out to them that such a light wouldn't move the way the Spook Light does, they claimed the Spook Light didn't move either. It only appeared to move because of tree leaves and other foliage wafting in the wind.

Another popular early theory was that the light was some sort of luminous swamp gas or will-o-the-wisp. Some common-sense types suggested it was merely a light from a distant farm or from the town of Quapaw. The most common and most enduring scientific theory, however, is that the Spook Light comes from headlights on Old Route 66 over ten miles west of State Line Road.

This photo of Route 66 between Quapaw and Baxter Springs was taken in 1933, shortly after the highway was paved. *Courtesy of Vintage St. Louis and Route 66.*

An early convert to the headlight theory was Logan Smith, an employee of the *Neosho Times* who had lived in the Spook Light area for many years. He told A. B. McDonald, the *Kansas City Star* feature writer, in late 1935 or early 1936, that he'd seen the light many times and had studied it carefully. He took McDonald out to present-day E 40 Road and showed him how it lined up perfectly with a short stretch of Route 66 just east of Quapaw. (Leaving Quapaw headed toward Baxter Springs, present-day U.S. 69 or Old Route 66 runs at a northeasterly angle, but in the early days, according to Smith's description, the road briefly ran in an easterly direction and then turned north toward Baxter.) When McDonald objected that cars have two headlights while the Spook Light was just one light, Smith explained that any pair of headlights, viewed from a distance, merged into a single light. Smith dismissed the stories of those who claimed the Spook Light had been seen long before cars were prevalent in the area as mere fables.

One of the first people with a solid background in science to study the Spook Light was geologist and mineralogist Dr. George W. Ward, who came to Kansas City in January 1945 from the National Bureau of Standards in Washington, D.C. to help establish the Midwest Research Institute. Part of his duties involved speaking to various groups throughout the region, and while appearing in Joplin for a speaking engagement in April, a newspaper reporter related the story of the Hornet Spook Light to him. The story aroused his curiosity, and accompanied by the reporter and the publicity director for the institute, Ward almost immediately set out for the light to observe the strange phenomenon for himself. He and his companions parked on a gravel road (E 40 Road) facing west at the top of a hill that sloped down to the west for a long distance. Although his was an informal inquiry that did not receive newspaper coverage at the time, Ward described his investigation and the theory he developed as a result of his observations in a letter written ten years later. He said :

> Not long after our arrival a suffused glow appeared in the sky, to the west over a range of hills, the center of the light ted area being in line with the axis of the road. This was followed almost immediately by a ball of light estimated as 4 to 6 feet in diameter that appeared to descend out of the hills and to rapidly advance toward us.
>
> As the greenish-yellow ball approached, the Publicity Director of the Institute caused some amusement by exclaiming that he had seen enough and he dashed back to lock himself in the car. The light approached and seemed to envelop us. Upon rapidly turning toward the east to observe the continuance of the light past us, I observed nothing.
>
> After observing the phenomenon a second time, I placed an observer at these points: one in the center of the road, another some 50 feet behind him and one at the fence line off each side of the road. I was the first observer on the road and found that after the light passed me I could not see it, but that the observer 50 feet to my rear could still see it. The fence line observers reported only an obscure flash appearance. These observations then caused me to believe that the source of the phenomenon lay ahead to the west and preferably

over the range of hills. Further reasoning led to the possibility that the cause lay in the refraction of automobile headlights from a road in a direct line with the gravel road where we stood. The fact that the light did not always appear substantiated the refraction or bending of light idea in that the relative humidity and temperature would have to attain the correct values to produce density of atmosphere to bend the light sufficiently for observation. Further it was observed that as an observer moved down hill toward the observed source of light, the phenomenon was not visible while an observer remaining…at the top of the slope could see the light. The refraction theory was also borne out by the lack of good observation at the fence lines.

Ward's theory was notably different from Logan Smith's ten years earlier. Ward thought the Spook Light originated from the headlights of automobiles traveling Route 66 between Commerce and Quapaw on a stretch of road that was much longer than the one east of Quapaw that Smith described. Ward reached this conclusion despite the fact that he and Smith set up along the same road, present-day E 40. Ward said he formed this hypothesis after searching a road map for a road or highway that lined up with Old Spook Light Road, but he apparently made a mistake, because the road that runs along the north edge of Quapaw, not the stretch of highway between Quapaw and Commerce, is the one that lines up with E 40 Road. Perhaps his faulty conclusion stemmed from a too-cursory study of the map, or else his memory simply failed him after ten years. It's no doubt true also that the viewing road and the headlights road did not have to line up perfectly, but if Ward was looking due west along E-40, it's unlikely he was viewing car lights between Quapaw and Commerce.

After Charles W. Graham, the *Kansas City Star* writer, visited the Spook Light on a Sunday night in May 1946, he called on Colonel McCunniff at Camp Crowder the next day to try to interest him helping to determine the source of the mysterious light. His curiosity aroused, McCunniff readily agreed, and he assigned Major Thomas Sheard of the Signal Corps to head the investigation. In need of maps, Graham and Sheard were shown to the office of Richard Y. Jones, head of the civil engineering department. When they told him they were going to investigate the Spook Light, Jones grinned and told them the mystery had already been solved. He explained that he and Joe Duck, a friend of his from Southwest Missouri College in Springfield, had visited the Spook Light as early as 1930 and theorized that the cause of the phenomenon was car lights from a distant road, but they did not attempt to prove their theory at that time. After A. B. MacDonald's 1936 article appeared in the *Kansas City Star*, Jones and Duck went back to Old Spook Light Road, armed with a surveyor's transit, and concluded to their own satisfaction that the eerie light was indeed caused by headlights. However, they had never published their findings, preferring not to spoil the mystery for everybody else. Because of his prior knowledge of and experience with the Spook Light, Jones was recruited to join the current investigation.

Later that day (Monday), Graham took Major Sheard back to the place from where he had seen the Spook Light the night before. Using an engineer's transit, walkie-talkies, and the naked eye, they surveyed the lay of the land and identified some power poles and other landmarks in the distance to the west.

Graham and Sheard ate dinner at Hornet, where Jones joined them. The three then returned to the Spook Light area after dark but decided they needed to reconnoiter the area better before conducting their experiments. The next day, Paul Shields, a Neosho pilot, flew Graham to the Spook Light area, from where they surveyed the layout of the land from 500 to 1,000 feet in the air. Graham located a road on the far or west side of Spring River that lined up perfectly with the road from where he'd seen the Spook Light on Sunday night. As they followed this road, Graham saw that it ran straight for several miles and formed the north boundary of Quapaw.

He drew a sketch of the area, showing its roads and other landmarks. Then he and the pilot returned to Camp Crowder, where Graham, Sneard, and Jones made plans for the tests they intended to run the next night. Jones took charge because of having previously run similar tests. He worked out a system of signals and a precise time schedule for running the tests.

On Wednesday, the threesome returned to Quapaw to further scout out the area on both sides of Spring River. They were joined by an engineer in the Signal Corps, two or three other soldiers from

Sneard's command, two non-military men from Jones's engineering department, and two other civilians. After darkness settled in, the members of the group synchronized their watches so they could all adhere to the predetermined time schedule. Major Sneard, the signal engineer, and the two civilian engineers were assigned to the distant road west of Spring River that ran on the north edge of Quapaw, while Graham, Jones, and the rest of the group were assigned to two separate observation points along Old Spook Light Road. The investigative team then began carrying out the tests according to the prearranged time schedule and system of signals.

Engineer Richard Y. Jones at the transit, while other observers look on during the 1946 Camp Crowder experiment. *Photo from the Kansas City Star.*

The schedule called for Major Sheard to flash his headlights three times at 9:45 p.m., and those on the Spook Light road would answer with the same signal. A minute later Sheard would turn his lights on for two minutes, and the observers would answer in kind. At 9:50, two cars would be parked facing east on opposite sides of the distant road with their lights on. Five minutes later, the two cars in the

Sheard party would be parked on a slope one behind the other so that one set of lights would be above the other. At ten o'clock, the lights of one Sheard car would be covered with orange and the other with red cellophane. At 10:10 the two cars would be separated by about a mile on two high points of the Quapaw road with their lights on. After five minutes, the lights would be covered with cellophane as in the previous test. Sheard would then turn around and drive about five miles west on the Quapaw road. At 10:30 he would turn around and drive east flashing his headlights at intervals of about one second.

All the prearranged signals were clearly perceived by the observers on the Spook Light road at the exact time designated in the schedule. When the two Sheard cars were placed side by side, the light "blazed brilliantly." To the naked eye, it looked like one light, but through the transit scope two distinct lights could be seen. When the cars were placed on a slope one behind the other, the light looked as if it had suddenly broken in two, which, of course, was a phenomenon commonly reported by viewers of the Spook Light. Finally, when Major Sheard drove east along the Quapaw road for about six miles flashing his lights the whole time, the flashes were clearly visible to the observers the whole time except for a couple of brief moments when the car seemed to disappear behind dips in the road. Satisfied that they had confirmed with thorough testing the theory Dr. Ward had worked out the previous year, the Camp Crowder investigators packed up their transits and other equipment to go back to Neosho.

C. Paul Spidell, the man whose letter had initiated Graham's inquiry, witnessed the tests and announced afterwards that he was fully satisfied that the light seen on the western horizon came from car lights, but he said the tests did not account for the luminous tadpole or the wavering light with arms and legs that he'd seen scamper across a nearby field, because those phenomena occurred in a different location. Two nights later, the investigative team went back to the Spook Light area, and Spidell showed them where he'd seen the strange sights. All the investigators saw was a glow that looked like a dim light inside a frosted globe. They thought it could be foxfire or some similar natural phenomenon, but after two hours of waiting, nothing more spectacular appeared and they once again returned to Neosho.

Graham speculated that maybe luminous tadpoles and animated octopi only appeared to true believers. On a more serious note, he and his colleagues in the investigative team thought perhaps what Spidell had seen was an afterglow or after-image brought on from having viewed the bright light for some time and then turning away. They had proved a solution to the "mystery" light to their own satisfaction, but they did not want "to rob anyone of the enjoyment of a good ghost."

In early November of 1955, in response to an article published the previous month in the *Kansas City Star* about the Spook Light, a group of students from Shawnee Mission (KS) High School took a safari to northeast Oklahoma to study the Spook Light for themselves. According to the *Star*, they were "loaded with measuring, recording and communications paraphernalia."

Shawnee Mission High School students prepare to set out on their safari to study the Spook Light. *From the Kansas City Star.*

The students set up on Spook Light Road, and when the light appeared, it seemed to stay relatively stationary on the horizon, looking like a street lamp viewed from several blocks away. After studying the light through a telescope and doing other tests, the students concluded that this light was what most people experienced as the Spook Light and that it was indeed caused by headlights from Route 66, although the students identified a bend in the road just south of Quapaw as the likely spot of origin rather than the straight 4-mile stretch of road beyond the bend toward Commerce. The students did not see "the other type of light" that had been reported to them, "one which appears as a speck in the distance and rushes toward the observer," but they allowed that such a light might exist. Based on what people had told them, they thought it was probably caused by mine or swamp gases but that conditions would be right for such a phenomenon only two or three times a month, which would account for the infrequent appearance of this "other type of light."

After the results of the student experiment were announced in the *Kansas City Star*, a spokesperson for the Missouri Division of Resources and Development, which had been involved in promoting the Spook Light, wrote in to register his objection to the students' conclusions. He said the Spook Light had been there for 88 years, long before cars were in the area, and that car lights on a highway were constantly moving whereas the Spook Light was not. Bill Calvin, one of the organizers of the student outing, replied a few days later, explaining that the reason the Spook Light had been reported long before cars were prevalent was that any kind of distant illumination, such as a lantern or a house light, could show up in the Spook Light area the same way the headlights did. And the Spook Light, he said, was viewed as stationary only when viewed by the naked eye; when seen through a telescope one could clearly see a number of different lights creeping slowly along.

Bob Loftin conducted his study of the Spook Light in the spring and summer of 1955, and he published the first edition of his booklet about the phenomenon later that year. Although the main viewing area for the Spook Light had moved from E 40 Road to E 50 since the soldiers from Crowder had conducted their experiment in 1946, Loftin started by trying to replicate their findings. He found that headlights along a road on the north edge of Quapaw did indeed create a ghost light along E 40, but, since the primary viewing area for the light had switched to E 50, he wanted to see whether he could also find a road near the south edge of Quapaw that lined up with E 50. That's when he discovered the straight stretch of US Highway 66 running between Quapaw and Commerce. He was dubious at first that headlights from so far away, twelve or thirteen miles, could be seen on Spook Light Road, but a series of experiments using colored lights, similar to the tests the Army performed in 1946, confirmed for Loftin that Route 66 was indeed the source of the Spook Light along E 50. "There were times when only one car was moving east on the segment of Highway 66 and other times when 20 or 30 cars moved in this same direction simultaneously," Loftin said. "This explained why the phantom light would change from the appearance of a lantern to a stupendous ball of fire. The reddish glow of the light would vary as the number of cars and trucks increased or decreased as they moved in a westerly direction."

Because there were periods of time when the light was not visible, Loftin did not believe observers were looking directly at the light when they saw it. Rather, he endorsed the refraction theory that George A. Ward had first advanced back in 1945, and atmospheric conditions would have to be right in order for the light to bend in a such a manner. When those conditions were not right, intervening hills and woods prevented prospective Spook Light hunters from seeing the light along E 50 Road over ten miles away.

In 1959-1960, Carthage High School senior William E. Underwood, Jr. undertook a months-long study of the Spook Light for a science project that he planned to enter in a nationwide scholarship competition. With the help of friends and family, the young scientist conducted experiments similar to Gannon's and Loftin's using colored cellophane applied to headlights. When the car lights were flashed from a stretch of highway near Quapaw, Underwood saw the flashes through a telescopic lens on Spook Light Road eleven or twelve miles away. The Carthage lad failed to land a scholarship when the prize winners were announced in March 1960, but the results of his study were reported in area newspapers. When asked about the Spook Light being seen in 1903 when there was no motor traffic in the vicinity, Underwood said the fog from Spring River, between Quapaw and the Spook Light, could serve as a lens for any kind of light, including those caused by swamp gases. He also thought "imagination played a big part in the stories of the 'spook' light."

Los Angeles resident Raymond Bayless, an investigator of psychic phenomenon, made a trip to the Ozarks in October 1963 and stopped in northeast Oklahoma to see the Spook Light. One of the first persons to investigate the light from a paranormal perspective, he published his findings the following year in *Fate Magazine*, and his full report is available in the State Historical Society of Missouri's manuscript collection.

Before drawing any conclusions about the Spook Light, Bayless first offered a description of it. When he and his wife first saw the light as they looked down Spook Light Road with the naked eye, the orb was very bright but fluctuating in intensity and sometimes splitting into two lights, with a bright one appearing above and slightly to the right of a dimmer and lower one. Driving along Spook Light Road, Bayless found that the light would appear and disappear "due to the hilly nature of the road." And when he looked through Spooky Meadows's telescope, Bayless discovered that the light was not just one or two lights but at least four. His wife saw six distinct lights when she looked through the scope, and Meadows told the couple that he had seen as many as sixteen. The light did not move down the road or perform any other extraordinary feats while Bayless was watching it, but he still concluded that "the origin of the Spook Light is indeed a formidable problem."

Briefly describing some the natural phenomena that had been suggested as possible sources of the light, Bayless refuted each theory in turn as a solution to the problem. For instance, he said that will o' the wisp or jack o' lantern was simply not bright enough to be the Spook Light.

He then got to the main thrust of his investigation, trying to disprove the car light theory. Bayless mentioned some of the people who'd previously advanced such a hypothesis, such as George W. Ward and Bob Loftin. The author was rather vague in his summary of their findings, preferring instead to emphasize the inscrutability of the light. For instance, he said that the experiments of the army engineers who'd studied the light in 1946 "were not conclusive."

Bayless's argument against the car light theory centered around the many anecdotal stories he had collected of Spook Light sightings long before automobiles were prevalent in the area. One such story came from Arthur Holbrook, a car dealer in the Joplin area, who said he'd first seen the light in 1905, when there was a total of only about a dozen cars in all of Joplin. Holbrook also claimed he'd heard of the light several years before he saw it.

Leslie W. Robertson, co-curator of the Spooksville Museum, told Bayless he'd first seen the light in 1916, that he'd seen it thousands of times during the intervening years, but that he had never seen it over any other road besides the one where it now appeared.

Bayless cited statements from a two or three other elderly people who said they'd seen the light in the very early 1900s, as well as one from an 81-year-old man who said he knew of the light as early as 1892. At least a couple of witnesses, though, said they'd first seen the light 30 to 35 years ago (1928 to 1933).

In conclusion, Bayless admitted the car light theory was the most reasonable explanation that he had encountered for many of the Spook Light sightings, but he could not reconcile all the earlier sightings, prior to the automotive age, with this theory. "The lights," he concluded, "stay in part a mystery."

In 1965, Robert Gannon set out to study the Spook Light and try to determine its source for an article he was writing for *Popular Mechanics*. Gannon discounted the "swamp gas" and "will o' the wisp" theories because he said such phenomena would be insufficient to produce a light as intense and lasting as the Spook Light. Looking west from Spooky Meadows's museum, Gannon used a lensatic compass to triangulate three telephone poles in the distance along Spook Light Road where the light seemed to make its appearance. When Jean Prideaux, an instructor of mechanical engineering at the University of Arkansas, arrived with a telescope to help Gannon with his experiment, the two followed Spook Light Road about three miles until they came to a rise where the three telephone poles were located. When Gannon had viewed the Spook Light from near State Line Road, the V of the overhanging trees lining the road acted as a sight so that he could see only a single light in the angle of the V. Three miles down the road, though, the area was more open, and suddenly he could see numerous lights. Using the compass readings he'd gotten back at State Line Road, Gannon, with Prideaux's help, set up the telescope so that he would be looking in the same direction that he had looked when viewing the light from State Line Road. When he looked through the telescope, Gannon saw not one but several "spook lights" in sets of two that appeared to be "slowly crawling down the darkness in a wiggling, peculiar snakelike pattern. Sometimes there were only a couple of pairs; other times there were as many as eight, shimmering and vibrating as though shining through 'heat waves.'" The lights had the same "peculiar golden color" he'd noticed when he'd seen the Spook Light back at the state line.

"Seen with the naked eye," Gannon continued, "they blended into a single light, the brightness varying with the number. Through a pair of good field glasses, the light separated into a number of single dots." But when viewed through the telescope, they resolved into what looked like automobile headlights. Gannon counted 15 pairs of lights between 3:30 a.m. and 4:00 a.m.

To confirm the headlight theory, Gannon and his associate waited until daylight and, scouting out the area to their west, located a straight stretch of U.S Highway 66 over four miles long between Quapaw and Commerce that lined up perfectly with Spook Light Road. The nearest part of the highway was ten miles away from State Line Road. Gannon then put colored cellophane over the headlights of his car and drove to the section of Route 66 in question, leaving Prideaux back on Spook Light Road where they'd set up the telescope. Gannon drove eastward along Route 66 periodically blinking his lights, and when he and his associate rendezvoused, Prideaux reported that he'd seen every blink. To further substantiate his theory, Gannon contacted the Oklahoma Highway Department, and, based on previous traffic counts, they estimated that thirty-three cars, on average, drove eastward along the part of Route 66 in question each morning between the hours of 3:00 and 4:00. This matched up closely to Gannon's count of fifteen cars in a half-hour span between those two hours.

"Now that Spooklight's source has been found," Gannon asked rhetorically when his article was published in September, "have we ruined everything?" He then proceeded to answer his own question:

> Not at all. In the first place, even without a mystery the light is a remarkable thing, with all the critical factors that must come into focus: a long, narrow road edged with trees that exclude outside light, a road perfectly aligned with another road across a dozen miles of emptiness, yet at a slightly higher elevation, and a line-of-sight close enough to the moist ground for the effect of "heat waves"—layers of varying-temperature air—which accounts for the shimmering and the peculiar golden hue.

Besides, he said, most people familiar with the Spook Light weren't going to believe his explanation anyway. He cited Spooky Meadows as an example. "Maybe so," Spooky had drawled when Gannon told him of his findings, "but explain the fact that the light was seen in 1886. No US 66 then. No motor cars, either."

Springfield resident Robert "Bob" Gibbons first began studying the Spook Light as a high school science student at Parkview in the early 1960s. As a senior at Drury College in 1965, he presented a symposium on the light advancing the headlight theory. To make his argument, he used movies and slides of the light that he and an associate had been collecting since 1960. Gibbons said he'd heard fantastic stories about the Spook Light such as setting a haystack on fire, entering an automobile and burning the upholstery, or sitting on top of an old lady in place of her head as she walks down the road, but he dismissed them as "distorted accounts and deliberate lies." To the contrary, Gibbons said he'd never seen anything more spectacular than "a spot of light bobbing about at the end of the gravel road."

Gibbons explained that, when he looked at the Spook Light through a telescope, he could see "four distinct pairs of lights, with pairs of red lights appearing slightly to the right of pairs of bright white lights. The red lights grew dimmer as the white lights became brighter." Gibbons's observation, of course, is consistent with the idea of traffic moving east and west along distant Highway 66.

Then in 1969, as a physics instructor at Southwest Missouri State University (now MSU), Gibbons and astronomer Richard O'Neil led a group from Springfield, including SMSU students and members of an amateur astronomy club, on an expedition to once again study the Spook Light. Their equipment included a laser gun with a powerful red beam, which they borrowed from the college. The researchers split into two groups, one remaining on Spook Light Road with the laser while the other drove to Highway 66 just west of Quapaw. The group on Spook Light Road aimed the laser beam directly down the road toward the spot where the Spook Light normally appeared, and the group on the highway drove slowly east while flashing their car lights. Not only did the group stationed near the Missouri line see the flashing of the headlights, but the group in the car could plainly see the red glow of the laser beam. In reporting the experiment, Springfield newspaperman Joe Clayton declared that Gibbons and his group had "shot down an armada of UFO's right over Spooksville Airport" with their laser. "More factually, they blasted a myth which has puzzled, awed or entertained Ozarkers for half a century."

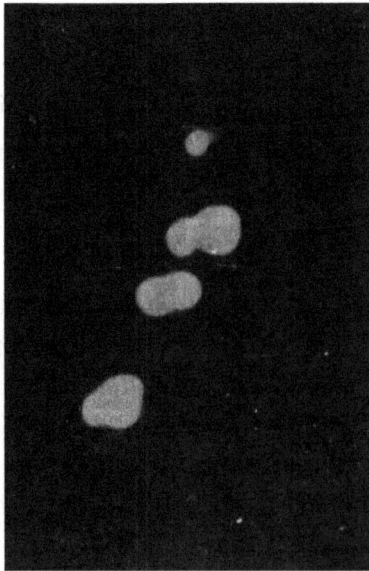

Photo of the Spook Light taken through an 8-inch reflecting telescope by astronomer Richard O'Neil in 1969. *From the Springfield Daily News.*

Clayton's tongue-in-cheek mention of Spooksville Airport was a reference to Bob Loftin's book *Identified Flying Objects*, which had been published the previous year. Although Loftin had been a proponent of the car light theory back in the 1950s and early 1960s, he'd apparently decided during the intervening years that the paranormal sold better than science. In the 1968 book, Loftin touted the fantastic notion that Spooksville was a UFO landing spot or filling station for alien flying saucers, suggesting that the deserted mine fields in the area, with their abundance of minerals, might be of particular interest to visitors from another planet and a logical place for them to set up a base of operations. "This," he concluded, "seems to be the most feasible answer to the mystery."

In advancing his argument, Loftin cited his own initial encounter with the UFOs of Spooksville in the summer of 1952. After Loftin had picked out a good observation point during the day, he, his wife, and another couple drove back to Spook Light Road that night:

> Almost immediately after the car rolled to a stop, we saw a strange light in the western sky. At first it appeared as a bright star, but as it came closer and closer, we knew we were in luck. The light seemed to come within about three city blocks of us before it disappeared. At the closest point the strange light from the UFO looked about the size of a locomotive headlight.
>
> After the UFO turned off its powerful light, I got out of the car to try for a better look at the now unlighted object…. A creepy feeling came over me as I stood there in the dark. I had just started to join the others in the car when IT HAPPENED! A bright light illuminated the car and the road around it as bright as day. I glanced at the occupants of the car, and saw a look of horror on their faces. Before literally diving back into the car, I turned to take a look at the source of the intense light. Approximately fifty feet behind the car, at an altitude of about 200 feet, a spotlight was shining down upon us from the sky above. We heard a noise, something like a strong breeze blowing through the trees—a kind of swishing or whistling sound.
>
> I could not determine the shape or size of the UFO because I was blinded by its searchlight. I jumped into the car and took off like a "turpentined" cat.

Loftin said that later, while viewing the mining area ten miles west of State Line Road through Arthur Meadows's telescope, he counted sixteen UFOs at one time flying in a straight formation. To further bolster his UFO hypothesis, Loftin then chronicled several extraordinary encounters with the light that other people had reported to him or that he had read about, and he mentioned Joe Clayton as among those who were mystified by the light.

When Clayton saw the book, though, he objected to his name being used to promote what he considered an outlandish theory. The newspaperman had indeed written about the Spook Light several years earlier, citing a motorist who approached the light until it vanished and then suddenly reappeared behind him. "The strange, glowing, floating ball," Clayton had concluded at the time, "remains one of the few things left on earth which defies all efforts to strip it of its mysticism."

But Clayton had taken an opposite path from Loftin and had converted to science during the intervening years. He admitted that he had written that "rich, beautiful prose, ...but to clear [my] family name, I must add that I followed up with another visit and a second article intended to strip away that 'mysticism.' Unfortunately, Mr. Loftin doesn't mention it."

About 1970, Marion Sloan and Herb Schade studied the Spook Light, using a telescope and other equipment, and they determined that it was headlights from Old Route 66. Both men were later longtime college professors, Sloan at MSSU and Schade at Crowder, and Schade was one of the consultants for the 1981 *Real People* episode about the Spook Light.

Following up on colleague Robert Gibbons's study of the Spook Light, SMSU physics professor John Northrip and some of his students made several trips to the Hornet area in the early 1970s with "lasers, walkie-talkies, and assorted gadgets to unravel the mystery" of the light. The group "determined that rising heat from surrounding hills was carrying light from a nearby highway, creating the dancing light."

During the first thirty-five years or so after the Spook Light's existence became widely known, Raymond Bayless's 1963 study was one of the few that approached the subject from a paranormal perspective, but during the past fifty years such studies have become fairly common, more prevalent even than those undertaken from a rational or scientific standpoint. Monty Blue Skelton, president of the North American UFO Organization, and Kevin D. Randle, director of research for the organization, carried out one such study in early 1977.

Among the equipment the pair used during their investigation were radiation detectors, a magnometer, an altimeter, and spectroscopes. The men had heard reports of UFO sightings in the Spook Light area, but they agreed that there was no connection between the Spook Light and the unidentified flying objects. Randle, in fact, was skeptical of the whole idea of extraterrestrial space travel, although Skelton was not.

What conclusions, if any, the two men drew from their study of the Spook Light is unclear. Many years later, Randle wrote in an online blog about his and Skelton's 1977 visit to the Spook Light, but he still gave little indication what he thought the origin of the light was. His statement that people around Joplin "are going to believe what they want to believe" seemed to embody his stance on the issue. He apparently didn't think it was up to "an outsider," as he called himself, to offer an explanation.

Dale Kaczmarek of the Ghost Research Society visited the Spook Light in the late summer of 1982 and again in the spring of 1983 to study the phenomenon. He published the results of his investigation in the July 1983 issue of the *Quarterly Newsletter of the Ghost Research Society*. After a rather strained attempt to discredit previous investigations, especially those that had put forth the headlight theory, he offered his own take on the light. Although he couldn't be sure what the light was, he was intrigued by the legend of a beheaded person looking for his head. Throughout the United States, he explained, "There are numerous examples of ghost lights appearing soon after some unfortunate person lost his head in some bizarre accident."

Kaczmarek also thought it possible that the Spook Light was the ghost of long-dead Native Americans whose burial grounds were disturbed when Spook Light Road was cut through the area. In addition, Kaczmarek considered it significant that the place where the Spook Light was usually seen had changed over the years. "This is not unusual for ghost lights to remove themselves from heavily populated areas and reappear in sparsely inhabited regions."

Kaczmarek preferred to view the light through powerful binoculars after 3:00 a.m. when there was virtually no other traffic along Spook Light Road. Describing one of his first encounters with the light, he said,

> When I caught it in the binocular field, it was a few feet above the ground and near a barn. At first I thought the barn was on fire or perhaps someone had a bonfire raging nearby. I was soon to discover that this was not the case. We were approximately 75 to 100 yards away and were in for a shock. The light appeared to be a diamond shaped object with a golden hue and a hollow center. You could actually see the trees and bushes right through it. It stayed in that area for about sixty seconds and then dropped behind a hill. The area where the light was a second ago still glowed with some kind of luminosity or phosphorescence. The area sort of twinkled with energy.

The light reappeared and disappeared behind the hill two or three more times. Then, after a few moments, when it failed to appear yet again, Kaczmarek crept up the hill in his car hoping to see where the light had gone. When he reached the top of the hill, the light was already a mile and a half away, and only a minute had gone by. "It displays incredible speed and cunning," Kaczmarek said, attributing anthropomorphic characteristics to the light. "It seems to know when someone is getting too close."

Kaczmarek was able to capture the Spook Light on film, and when he later showed the pictures to a clairvoyant associate of his, she said, "The light isn't a light but a doorway to another dimension," and she told him that he'd been in great danger fooling around with the Spook Light.

In 1986, Keith Partain, a laboratory technician from Tulsa, came up with a new theory on the Spook Light. He'd been studying the light since about 1979, when he saw an article about it in a Tulsa newspaper, and he had concluded that what most people saw looking west along Spook Light Road was indeed headlights from Old Route 66. However, sightings of the "real" Spook Light were rare, he said, because it only appeared, in the form of ball lightning, at ten or eleven-year intervals corresponding to the sunspot cycle.

This photo by Marta (Poynor) Churchwell was Keith Partain's initial inspiration for his ball lightning Spook Light theory. *Courtesy of Marta Churchwell.*

Partain's ball lightning theory first occurred to him after he saw a 1977 *Joplin Globe* photo by Marta Poynor showing the Spook Light with a connected filament shooting off from it. Since the ball of light and its filament appeared to be in front of the tree line, he didn't think it could be headlights from a distant road.

"Ball lightning is an unusual phenomenon that consists of a ball of charged particles of ionized matter," he explained. "But scientists do not understand how or why ball lightning exists, nor can they predict when or where it will appear."

Partain thought the Spook Light was restricted just to the general area of Spook Light Road but that it could appear anywhere in that vicinity. "When all you see is a little wriggle at the end of the road," he explained, it was just cars on the distant highway.

Of course, Poynor's photo was taken looking down the very road Partain was talking about, but he didn't explain that coincidence.

Harry Shipman, a professor of physics at the University of Delaware, admitted that Partain's basic idea that ball lightning could explain a lot of unusual sightings was reasonable, but Shipman doubted that "the sunspot cycle could be correlated with ball lightning in any one place."

In early April 1980, Tulsa resident and amateur investigator of strange phenomena Paul A. Roales, visited the Spook Light to see if he could determine its source. Arriving a couple of hours before dark, he looked west along the Spook Light Road through his 7 X 35 binoculars and could see the stretch of Old Route 66 west of Quapaw that those who posited the headlight theory usually identified as the likely place where the headlights came from. He could even see occasional glints of light reflecting from some of the cars as the sun set in the west. When the Spooklight Museum opened at 6 p.m., Roales visited with Spooky Middleton until darkness set in and then went back out to the spot where he'd viewed the highway that afternoon. Once again looking west through his binoculars, he saw that "the Spook Light was nothing more than car headlights" on Old Highway 66 about ten miles away. Occasionally several lights were visible at the same time through his binoculars but would merge into one when viewed with the naked eye. He theorized that the presence of more or fewer cars on the highway accounted for the apparent brightening and dimming of the Spook Light when seen without magnification. When Roales published his findings online years later, he received numerous messages disputing his conclusion, but he stuck by his findings. Yes, the Spook Light was seen before cars were prevalent, he admitted, but very seldom, and the rare instances could be accounted for by other kinds of lights such as lanterns or campfires. Why, he asked, is the light always seen in the same location in the V of the trees overhanging the viewing road if it is anything other than car lights coming from a highway that lines up perfectly with that road? When one person protested that the Spook Light couldn't be headlights from Highway 66 because there was an intervening hill that would block out the car lights, Roales suggested wryly that maybe the hill had grown since his 1980 visit.

During the 1970s, 1980s, and early 1990s, Michael Persinger, a neuroscientist and geologist at Laurentian University in Canada, developed and expounded a theory positing that "tectonic strain" within the earth's crust caused luminous phenomena. Tectonic strain has since been suggested as an explanation of the Spook Light, but it's unclear whether Persinger himself ever specifically studied or applied his theory to the Hornet light.

The December 1990/January 1991 edition of *Exploring the Unusual*, a newsletter of the Heritage Institute for Psychic Research, contained an article chronicling two visits that astronomer William Powers of Northwestern University and an unnamed associate made to the Spook Light many years earlier, and it gave the conclusions they reached from on-the-ground observation with the naked eye. One of the pair (not clear which) had accompanied members of the Condon Committee to the Spook Light in 1967. (The Condon Committee was a project funded by the United States Air Force at the University of Colorado in the late 1960s to study UFOs.) After the Spook Light appeared, the investigator walked down the road toward it. It disappeared as he started down a slope but reappeared when he backtracked to his starting position. He and his Condon Committee associates then got into a car and started down Spook Light Road. The light kept disappearing as they drove into the dips in the road but reappearing at the tops of the hills. After driving about 2.7 miles down the road, they came to a place where the light, along with a lot of other lights, suddenly appeared. They concluded that the Spook Light was nothing more than one of many lights coming from a distant town, which they misidentified as Miami, Kansas. (Now that would have been a supernatural phenomenon indeed, for lights from Miami, Kansas, to be seen in northeast Oklahoma, since there is no Miami, Kansas, unless you're talking about the county.) The investigators apparently meant Miami, Oklahoma, but that, too, of course was a misidentification.

In 1971, Powers and his associate returned to the Spook Light for a second visit to verify their findings. In the 1990-1991 newsletter, the associate described the conclusion he reached:

> There remains in my mind no question of the natural cause of these lights. Examination of the terrain shows that the sight from the initial sighting point grazes three rises in the road, perhaps even as closely as a foot. The crests of the hills form, thus, a series of 'knife edges' along the line of sight, a perfect setup for the exhibition of light refraction.... I remember putting my eye progressively closer to the ground at the initial sighting point; the lights disappeared. Had there really been a little old bald headed man coming up the road carrying a lantern, his lantern would have remained visible.

A Mensa group from the Joplin area ventured out to Spook Light Road one night in the late summer of 2000. The Mensas (members of an international high IQ society) wanted to view the light not so much with an intent of solving its mystery but just for "a little intellectual fun." Alas, the cagey light failed to make its appearance, and an article by Max McCoy about the group's expedition appeared in the *Joplin Globe* a few days later entitled "Spook Light Outwits Geniuses."

In the summer of 2002, Dale Kaczmarek, who'd studied the Spook Light in the early 1980s, returned with a team from his Ghost Research Society and set up on three consecutive nights along Spook Light Road, armed with night vision video cameras, a Geiger counter, a negative ion detector, and an electromagnetic field meter. The high-tech equipment proved of limited benefit because, according to Kaczmarek, the devices have a limited range, and the light never got close enough. The first night the group didn't see the light at all, but the second night two members of the team saw a purplish light that stayed at treetop level for about fifteen seconds, which Kaczmarek thought might be the Spook Light, although he'd never heard it described as being purplish in color before. The third night was "payday," according to Kaczmarek. About 1:00 a.m. the team saw a pinpoint of light high above the road in the far distance. Whitish with a tinge of yellow, the light approached but lasted no longer than thirty seconds before disappearing. It repeated its routine a number of times with intermissions of several minutes between acts. Kaczmarek and his team watched the show for several hours, even capturing a few seconds of it on night vision video.

Troy Taylor, paranormal researcher and founder of the American Ghost Society, visited the Spook Light three different times in the late 1990s but failed to see the phenomenon on any of the three occasions. In December of 2005, he came back leading an American Hauntings ghost hunt, and on the night of the group's visit to the Spook Light, it accommodated the ghost seekers by putting in a brief appearance in the wee hours of the morning. Taylor, who wrote about the 2005 visit in his book *So, There I Was*, concluded that the Hornet Spook Light was "one of America's greatest mysteries."

Chapter 4
Close Encounters of the Spooky Kind

Tens of thousands of people have viewed the Spook Light over the years, and very few have come away with the exact same impression of the phenomenon. This chapter catalogs various individuals' brief observations about, descriptions of, and experiences with the Spook Light, related mostly in their own words. The testimonies are arranged generally in chronological order, from oldest to most recent.

"Heavenly day! Did you see that? What an eerie thing. It makes the gooseflesh creep all up and down my back."—*An unidentified young woman upon seeing the light for the first time in December of 1935 or January 1936.*

"To our minds, there isn't any mystery about the light. It's an electric light in the town of Quapaw, to the west down there, about five miles…. It just seems to dance around, and that comes from waves in the air."—*Clara Mae Goodeagle Shears, a Quapaw woman who lived along current-day E 40 Road in January 1936.*

"I've been studying it for four years, and the more I watch and study it, the more puzzled I am about it. Nobody knows what it is."—*Mr. Tracey, who also lived along E 40 Road in January 1936.*

"It couldn't be. That light is only a block away and you don't hear a motor."—*An unidentified Spook Light spectator arguing against the headlight theory in the summer of 1946.*

"It would just bounce around out there and keep me awake at night. You know, like someone would be out there with a big ol' light, and sort of waving it around."—*Bill Youngblood, a former resident of the Spook Light area, describing the light in 1955.*

"[I] turned around and there it was just a'sitting there on the back of the car. It throwed off a good bit of light, like an electric bulb close up to you. I took off in one big hurry."—*Gregory Briones, Seneca, relating in 1955 an experience he had with the light one morning about 3 a.m.*

"What we saw could not have been car lights. It might have been lights from the power plant at the river but no car light could float and hover over trees and fade like a soap bubble. Once it came up the road right toward us, the size of a baseball and reddish."—*J. W. Pouliot, who traveled to see the Spook Light after reading an article in the Kansas City* Star *in October 1955 suggesting it might be headlights.*

"I first saw the 'Spook Light' back about 1911, before many cars existed in this area. I have seen it a number of times, even in rain and snow and at all hours of the night for the past 44 years."—*Ora C. Winfrey, Redings Mill, quoted in Bob Loftin's 1955 booklet.*

"I don't tell them anything [about the light]. If they don't believe it, it's here for them to see for themselves."—*L. W. Robertson, who ran the Spook Light Museum in partnership with Spooky Meadows for a while during the early to mid-1960s.*

"There was the time when the ghost light got on a school bus, and the kids like to have turned the bus over getting off. Some of them jumped off the bus and ran."—*Warren Harmon, who also helped out at the museum during the mid-1960s.*

"It is disappointing to view the light with only the naked eye, as it appears to be just a pinpoint of light growing brighter, then fading away only to appear again. It should be viewed through a pair of good binoculars or a telescope."—*Madalin Marshall, who was a among a group who made a special trip from Kansas City to view the Spook Light in 1966.*

"Everybody knows what the Spook Light is. It's a light, of course. But the mystery is—what causes it?"—*Arthur "Spooky" Meadows, 1969.*

"The light was so bright that it temporarily blinded the driver and he had to stop the bus. Just as we stopped, the light went away."—*Louise Graham, circa 1970, recalling a time when the Spook Light perched on the rear window of a school bus she was riding on her way home from a school carnival at Quapaw. This was likely the same incident Warren Harmon had told about in the mid-1960s.*

"Seems the old light felt real neighborly one night and decided to help me with my plowing. I couldn't see too well, and I guess the old light sensed it, because he started hovering all over the field where I was plowing."—*Quapaw farmer Chester McMinn, circa 1970, describing an encounter he had with the Spook Light one time when he decided to plow at night because it had been so unbearably hot during the day. McMinn said he appreciated the help until the light darted toward him real fast and he "froze stiff," but then it drifted away.*

"Numerous such spook lights haunt this planet, and so far all attempts at scientific explanation of their source or origin have been unsuccessful. Experts have tried to explain the phenomena away by using the existing structure of orthodox physics. But, if we are ever to truly understand these mysterious fires and lights, we will have to go outside the existing framework to find the answers. For these ghostlights seem to shine directly from a world that transcends the material plane."—*Brad Steiner, in Occult Magazine, 1970.*

"I don't know how the light got there. It just did. It was a ball of fire. After getting behind us the light became two separate balls of fire, one immediately on top of the other. They were about a block or so away. The balls got together, I don't know how, and then it disappeared."—*An unidentified resident of the Spook Light area in 1976, describing a time some years earlier when they saw the light hopping down the road like a person dribbling a basketball and then it disappeared and reappeared behind them.*

"The light was sitting right at the back of my mailbox. It was bigger than a basketball. It stayed in one place for about an hour and a half. During the time, I was trying to get nerve to get wood for the stove. After about an hour and a half, I looked out and it had moved about 100 yards down the road."—*Another unidentified resident of the Devil's Promenade area in 1976, relating a similar experience that they'd had a few years earlier.*

"I don't think we were really convinced of anything to tell you the truth. We probably did just see car lights. We probably didn't even see the darn spook thing."—*Simpson Yeomans in 1981, recalling the investigation of the Spook Light he and his Shawnee Mission High schoolmates had undertaken 26 years earlier.*

"We drove a horse and buggy from Dessa 25 miles south of here to look at this light. I got quite a kick out of it; it was jumping around out of the timber."—*Garland "Spooky" Middleton in 1981, recalling the first time he saw the Spook Light 43 years earlier.*

"I was born right across the highway. I've never seen it. I don't believe in it. You've got to be either drunk or crazy to see it, and I'm neither."—*An unidentified woman who lived in the area of the Spook Light in 1981.*

"I haven't figured out what the Spooklight is, but I am quite willing to say what I believe it isn't. It's not headlight reflections.... It's not swamp gas, foxfire or will-of-the-wisp.... Ball lightning? No, much too rare."—*Dale Kaczmarek of the Ghost Research Society, 1983.*

In this 1984 photo, the Spook Light appears as two separate lights, a common phenomenon reported by numerous observers. *Photo by the author.*

"I've lived here for 28 years and have never seen the Spooklight. In my opinion the light is just an excuse kids use to come down on lover's lane. They drink, take drugs, and beat up on each other."—*An unidentified resident of the Spook Light area, in 1983.*

"People would rather believe crap than believe the truth. It's human nature to believe in the supernatural."—*Marion Sloan, professor of physics at MSSU in 1983, speaking of those who refuse to accept the headlight theory.*

"I imagine most of them wouldn't like to see it explained too well."—*Harlan Stark, Neosho Daily News reporter in 1986, commenting on the fact that many area residents liked to take out-of-town guests to see the Spook Light and were fascinated by its mystery.*

"It would appear and disappear as we watched it. The color changed randomly and gradually from red, through yellow, white and orange. The only disappointment was that it never came and sat on our car. In fact, it always appeared to be miles away."—*Chicago resident Jack Schmidling, in 1988, describing the Spook Light when he first saw it several years earlier while visiting relatives in the Neosho area.*

"The Spook Light is nothing other than a continuously changing combination of head lights and tail lights which, when seen at a great distance, appear as a single light whose intensity and color varies as a function of the traffic flow on the short section of Interstate 44 that it is visible from various spots along Spook Light Road."—*Chicago resident Jack Schmidling, in 1988, describing the Spook Light as he perceived it after viewing it through a 25X spotting scope during his second trip to Spook Light Road shortly after his first visit.*

"When you are setting out there on a dark damp night and the light appears right in front of your car which it will do and fade out to a pin point you will change your mind. I have seen it many times and the color of this light is much different from a headlamp on a car."—*Russell Coffman, Neosho, in rebuttal to Jack Schmidling.*

"It could be a flashlight for all I know."—*Noel Grisham in 1997, when he lived a mile or so off Spook Light Road.*

"I don't really know what it is, and I hope they never find out. It would spoil the mystery."—*Joe Smith, president of the Quapaw Bank in 1997 and a lifelong resident of the Spook Light area.*

"We had two carloads down there and we hadn't seen anything. And I thought, well, I don't believe it anyway. And then here it came down the road. It looked like the size of a basketball, and as it came toward you, it got larger. By the time it got to the second car it almost exploded. It was the size of the second car."—*June Smith, reference librarian at Joplin Public Library in 1997, recalling the first time she saw the Spook Light many years earlier.*

"I come from the Ozarks, so I'm used to the idea that, where there is a phenomenon like this, …stories have a tendency to grow like this."—*Physics professor John Northrip, in 1997, discounting reported Spook Light sightings from the late 1800s.*

"The best explanation I'd give is that it has to be some type of atmospheric optical illusion. But I can't explain it. I've seen it in clear weather, in cloudy weather, I've seen it in freezing rain, so it would have to be something constant in all those conditions."—*Ted Phillips, in 2000, who had previously worked as a field research associate at the Center for UFO Studies at Northwestern University and had studied hundred of UFO sites over the years. He then added,* "Any time you're looking down a long corridor—like in the case of the Joplin light—you're setting yourself up for optical trickery."

"I've seen it looking like a small, swinging light by the side of the road, a long distance away. I've seen it looking like a flaming ball burning down the road and one time—and I swear this is not an exaggeration—it came up to the front of the car I was sitting in. It was very bright; it was big like a basketball.… I as like: 'Lemme out of here.'"—*Duane Hunt, retired Missouri Southern State College professor, in 2000, recalling with a laugh all the times he'd seen the light over the years, going back to the 1940s.*

"Nobody knows what it is. There are just some things in this world that won't ever be explained."—*Jennifer Lunsford, member of a Native American family who'd seen the Spook Light on numerous occasions, speaking in 2002.*

"I just rack it up to being some kind of unnatural source. I wouldn't pretend to guess what it is."—*Barbara Kyser-Collier, mother of Jennifer Lunsford, also speaking in 2002.*

"The second we turned onto the road, we noticed a small light way off in the distance. Looked miles and miles away. We kept driving up the road at idle speed, all the while the light changing colors, moving, disappearing, reappearing, and changing size. Sometimes the light had a reddish color to it, sometimes a greenish glow, and sometimes it looked white. After about an hour of being out there we came over a hill and a white-yellowish basketball-sized light was at the bottom of the hill not more than seven feet from our vehicle.... To the side of the light I could swear there was almost a purple haze to the right. The light got about three feet from the car, then spun around in a two-foot circle parallel to the ground. We all got scared and had the car in reverse at full speed in no time flat."—*An unidentified individual relating in 2002 an experience he and some of his friends had in the summer of 1998, when the person was a student at Pittsburg (KS) High School.*

"On this particular night..., we saw the light up close and personal. We were sitting in my 1966 VW bug, watching it float around in front of the car, just fascinated at what we were seeing when all of a sudden, the light broke into 3 separate balls of light! It went under my car and came out on the driver's side. The 3 lights seemed to swirl around and around...they were kind of a yellowish color, then they flew back under the car and came out on Cindy's side and did the same thing. Then they flew back under the car, came out to the front of the car, the 3 merged back into one ball of light and it flew at a high rate of speed down the road."—*Melody in New York, in 2007, recalling a November night thirty years earlier when she and a friend saw the Spook Light perform some unusual antics.*

"I kept thinking I saw it but then realized it was house lights. I could definitely feel a lot of energy down those roads though. My adrenaline was going the whole time."—*Lily K, Springfield, speaking of her unsuccessful attempt to see the Spook Light in early January 2013.*

"We both saw this glow…from the road, shining upwards. It highlighted a tree overhanging the road."—*David Glidden, filmmaker and paranormal researcher, in 2018, recalling a visit he and an associate had recently made to the Spook Light area in a futile effort to capture the mysterious sphere on film.*

"The only way anyone ever sees the Spooklight is through the bottom of an empty bottle."—*An anonymous resident of the Spook Light area in 2021*

"In the late 70s or 80s, I met with a group of Parkwood biology students one night on the east-west road, gravel at the time, in the Hornet community where the spook light was known for being spotted. We met at the nearby eerie Spookhouse Museum before going about 1/2 mile down the road. A couple of people set up scopes and aimed them toward the west where the road went up a hill in the far distance. For the next few hours we watched different colored lights in the distance, several miles away, go together, separate, disappear, etc. My thoughts are that we were watching cars coming and going on different roads in the distance, and that the air varied in temperature as it flowed in and out of the hollows and affected the images of the lights. Much to everyone's dismay, we did not see any notorious balls of light bopping up and down on our cars and about the woods. The kids had lots of snacks so they had a fun, zany evening."—*Frankie Meyer, 2022.*

"My family moved to Seneca when I was 12 years old. As one can imagine, there wasn't too much for teenagers to do in such a small town, so my friends and I frequented the Spooklight. This was the early-to-mid 1990s, so it was still a country dirt/gravel road at that time (unlike today). I literally have no idea how many times I went to Spooklight road, but I know it was a lot, likely dozens of times over the course of the five years I lived in the vicinity.

"Nothing particularly spooky happened during my visits, but I always saw the light and whoever was with me always saw it, too. In fact, my best friend at the time used to tell people who hadn't seen it to go with me because they would then see it. And they did.

"We always stayed in our vehicles when we visited. Sometimes it would be busy, other times we'd be the only people there. Usually, we pulled off on the side of the road, sat in silence, and waited. After a while we'd see a light in the distance. It would move around, sometimes split then come back together. I don't think it was always the same size or the same color, either, but it was always interesting!

"One of the stories I recall hearing is the light represents a lantern being carried by a spirit in search of something or someone. Other than the times when I saw it split then come back together, that's an accurate way to describe how the light moved, very like someone walking with a lantern held out to light their way.

"Regardless of the reason for the light, I don't recall any negative experiences while viewing it, though we no doubt spooked ourselves from time to time.—*Jill Halbach, 2022*

Chapter 5
The Spook Light and Me

I first heard about the Tri-State Spook Light as a young adult living in the Springfield area during the late 1960s and early 1970s, but the rare, vague mention of a strange light that appeared nightly near Joplin didn't have a strong enough pull to lure me 75 miles down I-44 to view the phenomenon. Soon after I moved to Joplin in 1974 to teach at Memorial High School, though, I heard or read several stories about the light, and I soon decided I had to see it for myself. What had been merely mentioned in passing in Springfield was an engrained part of the local lore in Joplin.

I finally ventured down to Spook Light territory one evening in the summer of 1975, shortly after I'd completed my first year of teaching in Joplin. The light was located in an isolated, hard-to-find area, and I had to ask directions. I decided to take what seemed to be the most direct route, State Line Road. Getting there via that route proved to be almost as spooky as the light itself. Wending my way down the narrow, hilly, gravel road, I arrived around the time the sun set at an out-of-the-way spot about four miles south of I-44 where Spook Light Road intersects State Line Road.

I was surprised to see that the so-called museum I'd heard about was a ramshackle building with peeling white paint, but I knew I was in the right place because the words "Spook Light Free Museum" stood out in black on the front side of the shanty. I'm not sure what the place had looked like during its heyday in the 1950s and 1960s, but now it presented a forlorn appearance. Outside, only some splintered boards of a broken-down platform marked the spot where Spooky Meadows had set up a telescope years earlier. And when I went inside, I saw that the newspaper and magazine clippings on the walls were faded and brittle with age. The only furnishings in the main room were a pool table, a couple of pinball machines, and an old-fashioned soda machine.

Like the telescope, Spooky Meadows was also gone, and Garland "Spooky" Middleton had taken his place, having acquired not only the museum property but also his predecessor's nickname.

Extending west from the museum into Oklahoma, Spook Light Road was relatively flat for the first few hundred feet before giving way to a series of valleys and hills. Along this level section of the road, Spooky Middleton told me, was a good place to view the light.

As darkness began to set in, the "museum" started coming to life. A teenage boy drifted in and dropped a coin in one of the pinball machines, and a couple of tourists came in to inquire about the best vantage point to see the famous Spook Light. Spooky told them what he'd told me, and I followed the visitors out the door. Getting back in my car, I followed them down the road and parked about a 100 feet behind them to await the appearance of the fabled light. Although I could dimly see the car ahead of me and the fields on either side of me, the thick foliage of the trees that lined the road enveloped us in an eerie darkness, and I decided the place was as ghostly as its name. But the mysterious light did not appear, even after complete darkness set in over the Ozarks countryside.

After waiting futilely an hour or so for the celebrated orb to show itself, I took my disappointment to the museum, where Spooky informed me that the weather was probably too mild. He told me the light was more likely to make an appearance on nights when the sky was overcast rather than completely clear. But not if it was pouring down rain, he clarified. Bidding him good evening, I vowed to try again and headed back to Joplin.

One cloudy evening a couple of weeks later, I came back to Spooksville, as Arthur Meadows had named the place, and I brought my camera along. I was alone on Spook Light Road as I placed the tripod on the hood of my car and set the camera's f-stop for a long exposure. The threatening weather had seemingly kept other curiosity seekers away, and I settled in for what I thought would be a long and lonely night watch.

My vigilance, though, was quickly rewarded this time. The sun had scarcely dropped below the horizon when a strange orange ball bobbed into view in the V of the tree line above the distant road ahead. It grew brighter and dimmer and then brighter again before disappearing altogether and then reappearing moments later close to where I'd seen it the first time. The orb didn't perform any spectacular antics for me like those that some previous observers had reported, but this was good enough, I decided, as I clicked away with my camera.

Happy to have finally seen the Spook Light for myself and hopeful that my photos would turn out, I soon headed back to the museum to share my wonder with Spooky Middleton and to prod him for more lore about the mysterious light. When I told him that I'd seen the light but it hadn't done anything extraordinary, he said that wasn't unusual and that the light only "performed" on occasion. Sometimes, he said, it would approach very near to a person as long as you stood still or retreated, but as soon as you started walking toward the light, it would reverse course and go back the way it had come.

When I asked him about the headlight theory, he dismissed the idea out of hand. He told me he'd seen the light himself many years ago when cars were rare in the area, and he claimed a person was just as apt to see it a three o'clock in the morning as ten o'clock at night when there was a lot more traffic.

So, what did he think the light was, I asked.

"I honestly don't know what that light is." He paused to ruminate a moment. "I don't think we're supposed to know," he finally drawled, seeming to suggest that the inscrutability of the Spook Light was divinely ordained.

Those first two visits of mine to the Spook Light in the summer of 1975 were the beginning an on-again, off-again fascination with the light that has now lasted over 45 years. During the late 1970s, I started taking out-of-town visitors to see the light. The first such trip came in the summer of 1976, when my wife and I took my friend Boyd and his family to see the light after they came to visit from the Springfield area.

An article I wrote for the September-October 1977 issue of *Missouri Life Magazine* chronicled that experience. Entitled "The Hornet Spook Light," the article began like this:

> It is a warm, clear night in late August. Accompanied by my wife, our son, and a friend and his family, I drive to an out-of-the-way spot several miles southwest of Joplin on a country road and park the car. "Well, this is it," I announce.
>
> We pile out of the car and stand peering down the road into the summer darkness. "I don't see anything," my friend says skeptically. "Are you sure this is the right place?
>
> "Just keep looking," I assure him.
>
> "Let's go home," my friend's four-year-old daughter whines. "This place is scary."
>
> "Shh!" her mother chides her.
>
> Several seconds of anxious silence pass, and then I see it. "There!" I exclaim, pointing down the road.
>
> "Where?" my friend asks dubiously. "You're crazy, man. I don't see anything."
>
> "Over here."
>
> He moves a few steps across the road in my direction. "Here it is!" he shouts enthusiastically as he motions to the others. "You can see real well over here."
>
> My friend has just seen the "spook light" of Joplin for the first time, and his reaction is typical. The spook light—or ghost light, as it is sometimes called—never fails to stir a sense of wonder and excitement in the first-time observer.

The article went on to relate some of the legends about and possible explanations for the Spook Light, just as most other articles ever written about the Spook Light have done. The story was accompanied by a strange photo of the light, taken by Marta Poynor and first published in the *Joplin Globe*. In the photo, the Spook Light appeared as a bright ball on the western horizon with a filament or string of light shooting off to one side, sort of like the glowing octopus that C. Paul Spidell had described to Charles W. Graham back in 1946, except this one was missing seven legs and wasn't running through any fields.

That *Missouri Life* article in the fall of 1977 was just the first
of several I wrote about the Spook Light in the late 1970s and early
1980s. I quickly followed up my first effort with a second article that
was published in December 1977 in *Modern People*, a national tabloid
similar to the *National Enquirer*. Entitled "Mystery Spook Light
Haunts Small Town," the second article wasn't much different from
the first except that, rather than taking a personal experience approach,
it was based mainly on an extensive interview I had recently done with
Garland "Spooky" Middleton. One of the illustrations for the article
was a photo I took of Spooky and his wife, Hazel, standing in front of
the Spook Light Free Museum, and another illustration was the first
good photo I ever took of the Spook Light.

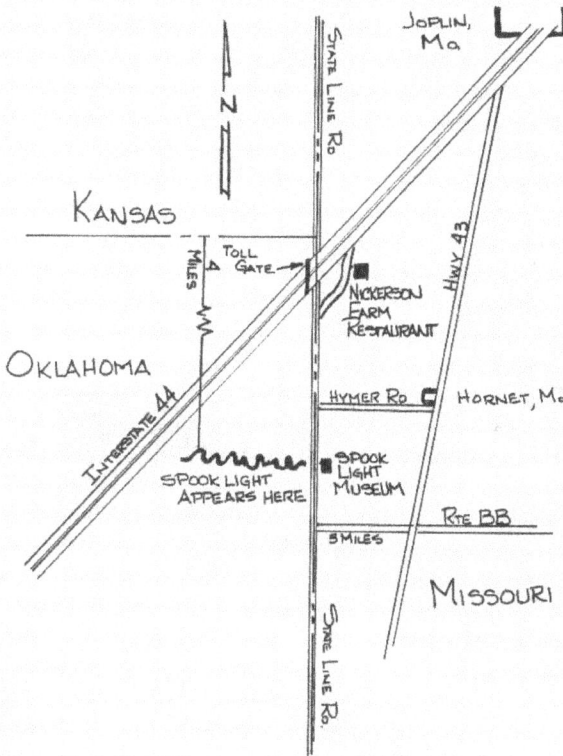

Hymer Road is now Gum Road, and the Nickerson Farms Restaurant is long gone,
but the basic layout of the Spook Light area is the same now as it was in 1977, when
this map appeared with my 1977 *Missouri Life* article. *From Missouri Life Magazine.*

Then, during the Halloween season of 1979, *OK Magazine*, a Sunday supplement of the *Tulsa World*, carried another article I did on the Spook Light. Called "Spook Light a Nightly Mystery," it had more or less a travel angle, aimed at getting readers of the newspaper to make the trip up the Will Rogers Turnpike to see the light for themselves. A photo I took of Spooky by himself outside his museum was used to illustrate the article, and that photo has since found its way onto the Internet, where it is often used in conjunction with stories about the Spook Light.

This photo of Spooky Middleton first appeared in *OK Magazine* in 1979. *Author's collection.*

While I was writing those three articles, of course, and for a couple of years afterward, I continued to visit the light and pay occasional visits to Spooky Middleton. During one of my later visits, Spooky, who was already well past retirement age, even offered to sell his "museum" to me. Although I was drawn to the Spook Light, I wasn't that fascinated by it. I knew that emptying coin trays from a couple of pinball machines each night and frying an occasional burger for idle teenagers wasn't a paying proposition.

A year or so after the *Tulsa World* article appeared was when I got the call from NBC's *Real People* asking for my perspective on the Spook Light. Not long after that *Real People* episode finally aired in 1982, however, a series of developments began to transpire that would gradually dull the light's allure for me. Spooky Middleton closed the museum in the summer of 1983, and he died less than six months later.

In the summer of 1984, just a few months after Spooky died, I wrote an article for *The Ozarks Mountaineer* lamenting his passing and bewailing the cheerless pall that hung over Spook Light Road after he was gone. Below are excerpts from the article:

> All is peaceful as I park my car on the lonely backwoods road known as Spook Light Road, which stretches westward on a straight line from the Missouri-Oklahoma border toward Quapaw, Oklahoma. The only sounds are the insistent call of a whippoorwill in a nearby woods and the far-off barking of a dog.
>
> It is a Tuesday evening in early June. The air is cool and refreshing after a hot, humid day, and the leaves of the surrounding oak trees waft gently in the mild, summer breeze. The sky has cleared this evening, promising a good night for viewing the mysterious phenomenon known variously as the Joplin Spook Light, the Quapaw Spook Light, or the Hornet Spook Light. I wait alone in the gathering twilight outside my car for the evening's first glimpse of the awe-inspiring light.
>
> A hundred yards behind me, at the corner of State Line Road and Spook Light Road, sits the vacant, dilapidated Spook Light Museum, closed to the public since the death of its proprietor, Garland (Spooky) Middleton. The "museum" …used to be a hang out for local youth. Now, though, it stands deserted, and a small sign warning prowlers and curiosity-seekers to "Keep Out" has superseded the one advertising "Open Nightly from 6:00 p.m. to 1:00 a.m."

Three other carloads of people wanting to see the Spook Light arrived over the next forty-five minutes that evening and parked along the road in front of me and behind me. The sparse numbers brought to mind the time Spooky had told me that 30 to 40 people normally visited Spook Light Road on an average weekday night, and I reflected that, at the rate I was witnessing so far, this night's total would not likely approach those figures.

The article continued,

Disrupting my reverie, a small, orangish orb bobs into view above the tree line as I peer down the road into the gathering darkness. It flickers brighter and then disappears, only to reappear seconds later. I am viewing the Hornet Spook Light for perhaps the 20th time, and yet it doesn't fail to excite a certain fascination in me just as it did the very first time I saw the mysterious light nearly ten years ago.

Still, something seems to be amiss tonight. With Spooky Middleton gone and the Spook Light Museum closed, visiting the Spook Light doesn't seem quite the same. Without Spooky here to embellish the story of the Spook Light with extravagant tales of its antics, the mystifying charm of the light seems somehow blunted. I ponder the thought that, when Spooky Middleton died without a successor to keep the "museum" operating, something of the legend and tradition of the Spook Light itself may have died with him. I suspect that the Hornet Spook Light will never again enjoy the reputation it once did…as a bona fide tourist attraction.

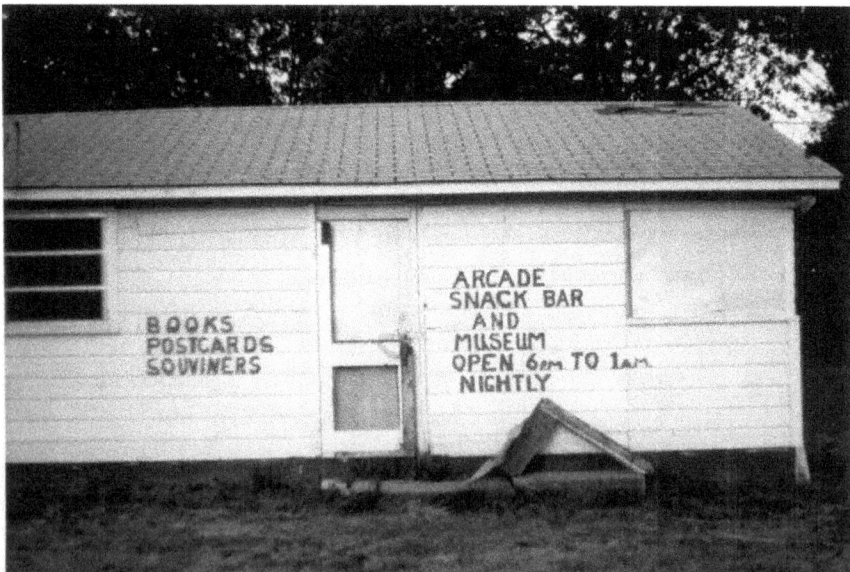

The Spook Light Museum had been closed less than a year when this photo was taken in 1984. *By the author.*

However, as I prepared to leave the Spook Light area that night almost forty years ago, I was buoyed by the thought that, as long as legends like that of the star-crossed Indian lovers abounded and as long as curious minds continued to speculate about the exact nature of the puzzling phenomenon, interest in the Spook Light might survive. And I ended the article on a hopeful note: "As long as there remain individuals such as those up the road ahead of me who have never witnessed the light for themselves, the magnetic pull of the Hornet Spook Light will endure."

Alas, though, events continued to unfold that would dim the Spook Light's glow.

About the time my *Mountaineer* article appeared, Leroy Potter, a fellow teacher in the Joplin Public Schools, took it upon himself to disabuse me of my fascination with the light. Leroy, who lived in the Hornet area and knew of my interest in the Spook Light, wanted to prove to me that the car light theory Bob Loftin and others had expounded was not just theory but actual fact. Leroy insisted I drive down to his house some evening, and he would show me the exact stretch of road where the headlights were coming from. One night I took him up on the challenge, and we drove slowly along Spook Light Road and eventually into Quapaw and onto Old Highway 66 headed toward Commerce. We had driven due west the whole time, except for a jog south and a similar jog back to the north. Although I wasn't certain we'd driven the exact distance south that we'd driven north, the stretch of highway between Quapaw and Commerce did seem to line up very well with Spook Light Road. I had to admit that Leroy had made a pretty convincing case.

After the summer of 1984, the Spook Light Museum continued to sit vacant a while longer, deteriorating even more than it already had. Eventually it burned down so that only a shell of the place remained. When new owners bought the property, they had no inclination to restore the "museum" but instead built a home on the site.

Then, not long after that, both State Line Road and Spook Light Road were paved, a Neighborhood Watch program was instituted in the area, and law enforcement officers started patrolling the vicinity more closely to dissuade vandalism and teenage parties. The entire Spook Light area seemed to lose some of its rustic appeal. Worse yet, the light didn't seem to appear as often or shine as bright as it had just a few years earlier. The Spook Light seemed, both literally and figuratively, to have lost some of its sparkle.

In 2005, I wrote yet another article about the Spook Light, this one for *Ozarkian Spirit*, a regional periodical published at Aurora for a few years. Among the people I interviewed for the article was Jay Rupar, another former colleague of mine in the Joplin Public Schools. A retired math and physics teacher, Jay proved to be even more of a skeptic than Leroy. Jay agreed with those who said the Spook Light was merely headlights, and he said he'd reached such a conclusion 40 years earlier when he took a telescope to the area as a high school student and viewed the light through it. Jay discounted the stories of the light having been seen long before cars were prevalent in the area as merely part of the mythology embroidered by Arthur "Spooky" Meadows and others to promote the light as a tourist destination. Jay thought the Spook Light had persisted as a mystery only because of people's inclination to believe in the marvelous. "It's no fun when people say it's just headlights," he explained, "even though that's what it is. Everyone wants a mystery."

Jay's unrelenting pragmatism left me feeling a little foolish for "believing" in the Spook Light. He told me I was doing a disservice even writing about it.

Not all the people I interviewed for that 2005 article, however, were as stubbornly rational as Jay. Mary West, a writer acquaintance from Springfield, told me she and her family had made multiple trips over the years to the Joplin area to see the Spook Light. "I'm no nearer to knowing the cause of the mystery light," she said, "than I was thirty-five years ago. It's what keeps us going back."

I next wrote about the Spook Light for an article that appeared in *Mysteries of the Ozarks, Volume 3*, an anthology published in 2011. For that article, I recounted some of the legends and theories about the Spook Light and then told of my own experience with the light, much as I have done in this chapter except in more summary fashion.

Following up on the quote from Mary West cited above, I ended the article with the following passage:

> The mystery of the Spook Light, or just the hint of one, is what keeps everyone else going back also to that out-of-the-way place ten miles southwest of Joplin, even today, with paved roads and all. So, I guess my friend Jay was definitely right about one thing. People do enjoy a good mystery. Even though I'm not as enthralled by the Spook Light as I once was, I, like Mary, still can't help being a little intrigued.
>
> The intellectual side of my brain tells me that Jay and the other skeptics who claim the Spook Light is nothing more than headlights are probably right; yet, there's a small voice inside me somewhere that's not so sure. Why, for instance, I ask myself, is the Spook Light harder to see nowadays than it was thirty-five years ago? There certainly aren't fewer cars on the road than there used to be.
>
> So, I guess I've come almost full circle. Where the Spook Light is concerned, I used to be a true believer, and then, at least for a while, I turned skeptic. Now I'm not so sure, and I've decided that maybe old Spooky Middleton was right after all. Maybe we're not supposed to know what that light is.

Most recently I visited Spook Light Road twice as I was writing this small book. Sad to say, I found that the light had lost even a little more of its luster since the last time I was there, for I was looking at the experience through the nostalgic lens of yesteryear rather than through the youthful eyes of discovery. On the first of my two recent trips, in October 2022, I tried but didn't see the light; at least, I don't think I did. I saw some sort of light in the distance, but it didn't look like the Spook Light I remembered, and there were two towers with flashing red lights along the road that didn't used to be there. The red lights shone above the road close to where the Spook Light has traditionally appeared, interfering with my ability to see the Spook Light distinctly, even if it was there. I tried to take a time-exposure picture of what I was looking at, sitting my camera on top of my pickup, in lieu of a tripod, to try to hold it still, but the photo came out looking like a blur.

Spook Light Road can still be an eerie-looking place at night, but none of the lights in this photo, taken in October 2022, is the Spook Light.

I went back to Spooksville again on a dark night in December 2022, armed with a tripod, but I still had little luck. I managed to get one picture that might or might not have been the Spook Light, but it still didn't look like the light I remember from the old days. It was lower to the ground, and I think it might have just been car lights from a couple of miles away..

This December 2022 photo, showing a speck of light in a black sky, might or might not have been the Spook Light. *By the author.*

I've talked to a few people who say they have clearly seen the light in recent years. They seem to be the exception rather than the rule, though, because I know of a lot of other people who agree with me that it's not as easy to see as it once was. All I know for sure is that, whereas I used to see it with regularity almost every time I ventured down to Spook Light Road, my recent trips to the area have largely been burnt runs. After my less-than-successful attempts to see the Spook Light in the fall of 2022, I came away feeling a little gloomy. Similar to the way I felt when I visited the place shortly after Spooky Middleton died and I wrote that nostalgic, backward-glancing article for *The Ozarks Mountaineer* in 1984. But now it's even harder to come up with a bright note to end on than it was forty years ago.

Chapter 6
So, What Is the Spook Light?

A number of articles written about the Spook Light, especially those written during the past 60 or 70 years, assert that the light was first seen in 1886. The truth of this statement cannot be documented, if by "documentation" one means written evidence. After extensive research of newspapers and other written records, I have concluded, as I noted in Chapter One, that the first written mention of the Spook Light occurred in 1934.

At this time, a few old-timers claimed, without giving specific dates, that they had seen the Spook Light many years earlier when they were young. For instance, one unnamed oldster said he'd seen the light "for more than half a century." Others claimed their parents or grandparents had seen the light in the 1800s. Still others said only that they had seen the Spook Light for several years.

In 1955, F. W. Mizer said the first time he knew of the light was 1903. This, as far as I know, is the earliest that the Spook Light can be specifically dated by firsthand testimony, and even Mizer was recalling an incident that had happened over fifty years earlier. In addition, he later admitted the light he saw in 1903 was not the same as the later ghost light seen on Spook Light Road.

The lore giving 1886 (or more vaguely, the late 1800s) as the date of the first sighting of the light usually also includes the assertion that the light created such a panic in the Hornet neighborhood that it caused many people to move away, including a Native American couple who blamed the deaths of their two children on the evil light. We know from A. B. McDonald's 1936 *Kansas City Star* article that at least part of this legend is dubious. According to McDonald, a man named Tracey, who lived on Old Spook Light Road at the time, told him he had purchased his home just four years earlier from an Indian couple who'd moved away because they blamed the deaths of their children on the light. This places the anecdote of the Indian couple moving away because of the evil light 46 years later than the date given in the legend. So, the story that has been handed down seems clearly to be a blending of fact and fiction, unless, incredibly, the same panic of 1886 was reenacted in 1932. Or unless Mr. Tracey was lying. And if part of the legend is exaggerated, it calls into question the rest of the story as well.

The significance of the 1934 date when the Spook Light first became widely known cannot be ignored, I think, because the paving of Route 66 between Quapaw and Commerce was completed just the previous year, and, as we have seen, many scientific investigations into the Spook Light have reached the conclusion that headlights on a stretch of Old Route 66 (present-day Alternate 69) are the primary source of Spook Light sightings. Highway 66 itself was completed about 1926, but it was not paved until 1933. Without completing discounting the old-timers' recollections of having seen the Spook Light many years earlier, we can legitimately ask, *If Spook Light sightings had been prevalent prior to the mid-1930s, why did the sightings only arouse widespread excitement after Route 66 was paved?* The obvious answer is that the sightings were probably rare until after the highway was paved. Also, the fact that a number of residents of the Spook Light area said during the mid-1930s that they had been seeing the light for "several years" seems to go along with the fact that the unpaved highway was completed circa 1926, because, if we hypothesize that headlights are, in fact, the main source of the Spook Light, it seems reasonable to assume that dust stirred up by automobiles on an unpaved road might well have obscured the headlights enough that sightings of the light were less frequent than they were after the road was paved. Also, presumably there was more traffic after the road was paved.

It is worth adding, too, that, although automobiles were rare in the Tri-State area prior to 1926, they were certainly not unheard of, even as early as the 1910s. So, some of the stories about Spook Light sightings many years before Route 66 was built may simply have exaggerated how long ago the sightings occurred.

In addition to the idea that the Spook Light created panic in the Hornet neighborhood when it was first sighted in the late 1800s, the legend that has been handed down usually also includes a statement claiming that efforts to explain the light have failed miserably. Assertions that "No one knows what that light is" or that "surveyors, geologists and scientists" have studied the light and come away baffled are common. For instance, Dale Kaczmarek claimed in the July 1983 edition of the Ghost Research Society newsletter that the Spook Light had "literally baffled researchers, scientists and investigators for nearly fifty years."

The study conducted by Camp Crowder personnel in 1946 is often specifically discounted in the story of the Spook Light that has been handed down. An official publication of the State of Missouri's Division of Resources and Development put out in the 1950s or 1960s and meant to promote the light as a tourist attraction said, in speaking about the military group who conducted the 1946 experiment, that "they came away baffled." Other writers have asserted that the Corp of Engineers concluded that the Spook Light was a "mysterious light of unknown origin."

Nothing could be further from the truth. In the first place, the Camp Crowder experiment was led by an officer of the Signal Corps, not the Corps of Engineers, although there were engineers involved in the study. More importantly, the Camp Crowder group, after perhaps the most thorough investigation of the Spook Light ever undertaken, stated conclusively that they were convinced that headlights on a distant road were the source of the mysterious light.

In fact, there is wide consensus among surveyors and scientists about the origin of the Spook Light. Virtually everyone who has ever studied it from a scientific perspective—from the Camp Crowder group, to the *Popular Mechanics* writer in 1965, to the researchers from Springfield led by physics instructors in the late 1960s and early 1970s—has reached the same conclusion: that headlights on Old Route 66 or some other distant road cause the mysterious light that appears on Spook Light Road.

So, both the fact that frequent sightings of the Spook Light were first reported shortly after US Highway 66 was paved and the consensus of scientific studies lead one to conclude that the large majority of sightings are, indeed, due to headlights. To those two proofs, we might also add common sense. If headlights do not account for most Spook Light sightings, why does the light almost always appear in the same location along the western horizon just above the tree line in the middle of the road? And why else would it disappear as one descends into a dip along the road but then reappear as one crests a hill?

Taken in total, the evidence seems undeniable that most sightings of the Spook Light can be accounted for by headlights.

But what about reports of the light pulling antics like landing inside a person's car and burning the upholstery? And what about those old-timers who claimed to have seen the light years before automobiles were prevalent in the area?

In regard to the extravagant claims of the light's outlandish behavior, I take the same position as Carthage High School student William Underwood back in 1960. Like Underwood, I think those stories are largely the product of over-active imaginations. Most people who've seen the Spook Light over the years, myself included, have never seen it do anything more extraordinary than grow brighter and dimmer and bob around a little bit. However, I do not completely discount the possibility that the light might, on very rare occasions, perform some sort of optical acrobatics.

As for the early reports of the Spook Light being witnessed long before cars appeared on the scene, I give them a little more credence. I don't completely discount such sightings as just part of the mythology spun by Spooky Meadows, as my friend Jay did, because there were many such reports predating Spooky's reign at the east end of Spook Light Road. However, I think such sightings were likely much rarer than the legend that has been handed down would have one believe. Like a few other researchers and writers before me, I think that the credible reports can be explained without resorting to the supernatural, because it is likely that the same conditions that allow car lights to be seen from over ten miles away might also be conducive to seeing lanterns, campfires, or other sources of light from a far distance.

If car lights are, in fact, the primary cause of the Spook Light, why have sightings of the light become rarer in the past forty years or so than they were in previous years? This one I don't have a good answer for except to speculate that the conditions that once facilitated one's ability to see a light along Spook Light Road that was coming from a long distance away have changed. For instance, Robert Gannon, the *Popular Mechanics* writer, pointed out in 1955 that part of what made the headlights from Old Highway 66 clearly visible along Spook Light Road, over ten miles away, was the tunneling effect that the overhanging trees above the road lent to the lights. In other words, the V formed by the trees above the road acted as a sight or tunnel to block out interfering light or other objects from view. Those of you who have been to Spook Light Road in recent years know that the V of the limbs overhanging the road is not nearly as clear or defined as it once was. Many of the trees along the road have been cut back or completely taken out, while others have branched out even farther over the road than they used to be. It's possible, too, that atmospheric conditions in the area have changed over the years, although that is admittedly pure conjecture. Also, there are those interfering red lights.

This photo from 1976 and the two on the next page from 1984 and 2022, all taken from generally the same spot, show how Spook Light Road has changed over the years. *All photos by the author.*

For whatever reason, the Spook Light is not as visible as it once was.

And I can't help feeling a little sad about that. No matter where the critter came from or where it went.

Bibliography

Books and Articles

Almeter, Curtis. "The Joplin Spooklight." *Joplin Toad*, October, 2021.

Bayless, Raymond. "Ozark Spook Light, A Scientific Report." *Fate Magazine*, September 1964.

Curtis, Skip. "The Spooklight." *Show Me Route 66*. Spring, 1988.

"Ghost Light of the Ozarks." *Ozark 71*. October, 1976.

Kaczmarek, Dale. "The Ozark Spooklight." *Ghost Trackers Newsletter*, July 1983.

Loftin, Robert. *Identified Flying Saucers*. New York: David McKay Company, Inc., 1968.

Loftin, Robert. *Tri-State Spook Light*. (Reprint, 1955). Joplin, MO: The Author, 1963.

Mysteries of the Ozarks, Volume 3. Edited by Ellen Gray Massey and Debbie Blades. St. Charles, MO: High Hill Press, 2011.

Polk, Deola. "Spook Light in Ozarks Gives Visitors Scary Show." *St. Louis Star and Times*, August 28, 1946.

Wood, Larry. "The Hornet Spook Light." *Missouri Life Magazine*, September-October, 1977.

_____. "The Hornet Spook Light: Can It Be Explained?" *Ozarkian Spirit*, Fall, 2005.

_____. "Mystery Spook Light Haunts Small Town." *Modern People*, December 4, 1977.

_____. "Spook Light A Nightly Mystery." *OK Magazine*, October 28, 1979.

_____. "Spook Light Revisited." *The Ozarks Mountaineer*, September-October, 1984.

Miscellaneous

Flyer about the Spook Light, Joplin Chamber of Commerce, n.d.
Flyer about the Spook Light, Neosho Chamber of Commerce, n.d.
Spook Light Vertical File, Joplin Public Library.
Spook Light Vertical File, Neosho-Newton County Library.

Newspapers

Chicago Tribune, June 16, 1966.
Chillicothe Constitution Tribune, October 30, 1935.
Joplin Globe, numerous dates.
Joplin News Herald, various dates.
Kansas City Star, numerous dates.
Los Angeles Times, various dates.
Maryville (MO) Daily Forum, October 12, 1959.
Neosho Daily News, numerous dates
Neosho Times, various dates.
Oklahoma City Daily Oklahoman, May 3, 1963.
Springfield Daily News, various dates.
Springfield Leader-Press, various dates.
Springfield News & Leader, various dates.
Tonkawa (OK) News, July 21, 1960.
Washington (MO) Missourian, September 22, 1955.
West Plains Journal, January 26, 1936.

Online Sources

Obiwan. "Hornet, Joplin, Seneca Ghost Light." *Obiwan's Ghosts and Paranormal*. Ghosts.org/hornet-joplin-seneca-ghost-light/.

Palmer, Sean. "The Hornet Spooklight." http://inamidst.com/ lights/ hornet.

Kaczmarek, Dale. "Joplin Spooklight Investigations." Ghost Research Society, https://www.ghostresearch.org/ Investigations/Joplin.html.

Randle, Kevin. "The Joplin Spooklight." *A Different Perspective.*

http://kevinrandle.blogspot.com/2006/09/joplin-spooklight. html.

Roales, Paul A. "The Hornet Ghost Light." Reprinted at *Astronomy Café* by Sten Odenwald. http://www.astronomycafe.net/ weird/lights/hornet1.htm.

Taylor, Tony. "The Hornet Spook Light." *Unexplained America.* http://www.prairieghosts.com/devprom.html.

Weiser, Kathy. "Devil's Promenade and the Hornet Spook Light." *Legends of America.* https://www.legendsofamerica.com/ mo-spooklight/.

www.ingramcontent.com/pod-product-compliance
Lightning Source LLC
Chambersburg PA
CBHW071620040426
42452CB00009B/1417